The Magic Years of
Beatrix Potter

'More than thirty years ago Margaret Lane wrote *The Tale of Beatrix Potter* [in Fontana], which ranks high among the biographies of our century. Now the great archive of Beatrix Potter's drawings, letters and diaries (more than 200,000 words in code) has drawn her back to her favourite theme, which is also one of mine.

'This is a biography with a difference . . . the emphasis this time is on the evolution of Beatrix Potter's art and its translation into some of the greatest books for children.' A. J. P. Taylor, *Observer*

'Margaret Lane is among the most accomplished authors of our time.' Raymond Mortimer, *Sunday Times*

THE MAGIC YEARS OF
BEATRIX POTTER

by
MARGARET LANE

FONTANA/COLLINS

First published in 1978 by
Frederick Warne (Publishers) Ltd: London
Frederick Warne & Co. Inc: New York

First issued in Fontana Paperbacks 1980

This book was designed and produced by
George Rainbird Ltd
36 Park Street
London W1Y 4DE

Design: Pauline Harrison
Index: Penelope Miller

Printed in Great Britain by
W. S. Cowell Ltd
Ipswich
Suffolk

*The frontispiece portrait is from a pencil sketch of
Beatrix Potter by her brother Bertram*

❧ CONTENTS ❧

AUTHOR'S ACKNOWLEDGMENTS

In *The Tale of Beatrix Potter* I made acknowledgment to a number of people who helped me some thirty years ago in my initial researches into the life of Beatrix Potter. For help with this later study I am indebted, as before, to Messrs Frederick Warne, and especially to their Chairman, Mr Cyril W. Stephens. I am also most grateful, for much assistance, to Miss Marjorie Moore, whose personal recollections of Beatrix Potter were invaluable; to Miss Anne Emerson of Warnes; to Mrs Anne Clarke of the National Book League, which owns part of the Leslie Linder Collection of Beatrix Potter material; and to Miss Joyce I. Whalley of the Victoria and Albert Museum, which possesses some two thousand items from the Leslie Linder Collection. Mr John Hadfield and Miss Georgina Dowse, of Messrs Rainbird, have provided invaluable help in research and illustration, and I have had generous co-operation from Mr and Mrs James Taylor, the Custodians of the Beatrix Potter Museum at Hill Top (it was Mrs Taylor who recently discovered a hitherto unknown Potter family photograph album which has provided us with many illustrations), and from other officials of the National Trust, especially the Regional Information Officer at Ambleside, Mr C. J. Hanson-Smith. Other people who have been most helpful include Mrs Emma Beck, who spent weeks sorting the Linder material in the Victoria and Albert Museum; Mr B. R. Curle, in charge of Local Studies at the Kensington and Chelsea Borough Library; and Mr Derrick Witty, who photographed much of the illustrative material.

I also acknowledge the courtesy of Hamish Hamilton Limited and Alfred A. Knopf Inc. in allowing me to reprint an essay from my book *Purely For Pleasure* which they published.

ᘒ Introduction ᘓ

It is more than thirty years since I began to explore the life and achievement of Beatrix Potter; even longer since I made my first timid (and ludicrously unsuccessful) attempt to approach her. Her little books had been the joy of my childhood; I had shared my delight in them with my own children, and had long recognized that my vision of the English countryside – its woods, farmyards, cottages, gardens, its domestic and wild animals – had always been deeply influenced by her innocent and apparently unsophisticated art.

I say 'apparently' unsophisticated because there is a great deal in Beatrix Potter's writing and illustrative art which is shrewd, ironic,

Rupert Potter with Beatrix and Bertram on holiday at Holehird,
Windermere, when Beatrix was twenty-three

poetic or even profound – undertones which children miss, but which echo again and again in the subconscious as one grows older. As an artist she follows, at her own modest level, the school of Bewick and Constable. Her best writing is simple and direct, with never a superfluous word; at all levels it carries a deep imaginative conviction. Her rabbits and hedgehogs and foxes, though they may walk on their hind legs, drink camomile tea and wear aprons or mufflers, are true to the last syllable to their animal natures.

This rare quality which she possesses is now recognized in many parts of the world to a degree which would have astonished her. Her little books are translated into many languages, even Japanese – she has become, I am told, a cult figure in Japan – and her animal characters have passed into our mythology. An impressive amount of study and research has been given to her work in recent years, chiefly by that remarkable and dedicated Potterphil, the late Leslie Linder, whose masterpiece was decoding and transcribing her 200,000-word secret journal, a labour which took him more than nine years. By now, everything that can be known, I think, *is* known; and yet one cannot help hoping for something more to shed light on the glimmer of genius in her work, and her unique character.

The history of her creative achievement is a strange one; perhaps the oddest thing about it is that her nineteen or twenty inimitable little books for children were all produced in the brief space of thirteen years. As an amateur artist, naturalist and secret chronicler she had worked absorbedly from her early childhood to her middle thirties, without discovering the true direction in which her talents lay. She had led a solitary and in many ways repressive life, a prisoner in the sterile habitat of her Victorian parents; so that it was not until, by a happy chance, she came to know the children of one of her former governesses that her work took the creative turn that was to make her famous. As soon as they could read, or even before, she began to write them little illustrated letters, telling the stories that were later to develop into *Peter Rabbit*, *The Tailor of Gloucester*, *Squirrel Nutkin* and the rest. She had found the audience to which her sympathy and imaginative gifts completely responded, and the letters and stories were received with such rapture by her childish audience that it is not surprising that eventually – another eight years, in fact, after the writing of the first letter – she began to think, with diffidence and modesty, of publication.

The story of her relationship with the publishers who at first courteously rejected her offerings and then (fortunately for themselves) decided to accept them, has been told in detail by Leslie Linder in his *History of the Writings of Beatrix Potter*. Frederick Warne & Co. became not only her publishers, but her friends; she began to pay independent visits to the family house in Bedford Square, and in the summer of 1905 became engaged to Norman Warne, the gentle and shy younger son, who had chiefly dealt with the little books and professionally advised her. This promise of a new and happier life was not fulfilled. Norman Warne died suddenly a few weeks later, and Beatrix Potter, now in her fortieth year, turned back to her books for children as the one creative impulse and expression left to her.

She continued for another five years to produce stories and pictures of incomparable quality, and then, it seems, the inspiration faded and the shy but secretly self-reliant Miss Potter turned into another person. Rarely, I think, has such a personality-transformation been recorded, but the causes are simple enough: her work, and a small legacy from an aunt, had brought her a certain measure of independence, and this independence led to the fulfilment of her interest in farming, and to a happy marriage.

Her parents had for a number of years been renting their holiday houses in the Lake District, and to this beautiful country of lakes and fells, dales and sheep-farms she responded with all the instinct of her north-country heredity. She spent her money in buying a little farm (ostensibly as an investment) in the village of Sawrey, and in the course of negotiations for the purchase became friendly with the gentle middle-aged Ambleside solicitor who conducted the sale, and – much against the wishes of her parents, as one would guess – happily married him.

From this moment Beatrix Potter, now Mrs William Heelis, lived another life, concentrated on her passionate interest in farming. True, she produced a few more little books for children, mainly because her publishers were understandably eager for them, but her time and energies were now dedicated to a very different existence, and at the age of fifty her eyesight was no longer good enough for meticulous drawing. Of these latter-day productions *The Tale of Johnny Town-Mouse* is the only one at all comparable with her best work. The rest are a hotch-potch of earlier experiments, or of little tales scribbled down at different periods and left, because of her failing eyesight, unillustrated. Most of these late productions were first published in America, in response to pleas from children's librarians, and from admirers professionally involved in what in that country has come to be known as 'kid. lit.'. Their letters of praise and entreaty were persuasive. 'I have always felt,' Beatrix Potter wrote towards the end of her life, 'that New Englanders understood and liked an aspect of my writings which is not appreciated by the British shop-keeper; though very possibly children the world over appreciate it, without consciously understanding that there is more in the books than mere funniness.' She knew that the quality of these final productions was far below her best, and for that reason insisted that they should not be published in England in her lifetime.

There is still, even today, a fair amount of Beatrix Potter's art work which has never been published, and which I saw first in 1943, going through her portfolios and wardrobe drawers with her widower, Mr

Heelis, in the little house in the village of Sawrey where she had lived for nearly thirty happy years. With the help of Mr Heelis and Beatrix Potter's surviving cousins and acquaintances, at last, in that year, I was free to unravel the story that had been so brusquely refused four years before when I had timidly written to ask if I might call upon her. From the age of fifty, when she entered her new province as solicitor's wife, sheep-farmer and conservative landowner, she had encouraged all that forthright, crusty and practical side of her personality which she had inherited from her north-country ancestors. Her little books for children belonged to the discarded past. Curious or admiring visitors were fiercely discouraged. She could intimidate rugged farmers or the judges at sheep-fairs, but at the same time, in the reclusive quiet of their own cottage, or rowing their boat on the tarn while William fished, or happily watching him as he nimbly went through the figures at country dances, she showed always an old-fashioned gentle deference to her husband and a respect for his way of life. The old life had been thankfully exchanged for down-to-earth work on the land and a happy marriage.

The last twenty-seven years of Beatrix Potter's life were intensely practical and productive, but not, in the earlier and almost magical sense, creative. It is in that brief remarkable period, from her mid-thirties to her late forties, that everything came into flower that made her famous. Remembering the muddled mass of unpublished drawings and paintings that I first sifted through so long ago in Sawrey, I have often wished to take a longer look at the scattered fragments and to trace the path of that happy self-discovery, of which they can tell us much. This is what I have now indulged myself in doing in this book, rather in the mood of someone pasting up a scrapbook. Here and there I have borrowed brief passages from my own earlier writings on Beatrix Potter, but for the most part have followed a trail through her journal and letters, often delighting myself with small discoveries, as I hope this leisurely ramble may delight others.

1

THE THIRD-FLOOR NURSERY

When Helen Beatrix Potter was born on 28 July 1866 at No. 2 Bolton Gardens, West Brompton, the houses in that quiet and prosperous area of Victorian London were all dignified, opulent and new. When the streets and squares were built in the early 'sixties it was on fields which had been owned and farmed by the Bolton family since the sixteenth century, and the infant Beatrix and her nurse, if they looked out of their barred windows at the top of the house, could still see fields and orchards as well as gardens. The roads were rough and could be very muddy in bad weather, requiring the attentions of crossing-sweepers at all seasons; it would be another sixteen years or more before a wood-block pavement would be laid in Bolton Gardens and a macadam surface spread on the carriage road.

It was an area successfully designed to attract prosperous middle-class families, who moved in, it seems, as soon as the paintwork was dry and the railings finished. The steps were whitened each morning by housemaids in caps and aprons, tradesmen descended the area steps respectfully, and in the mews behind the solid façade there were horses, carriages and coachmen.

Mr and Mrs Rupert Potter were certainly comfortably wealthy, both having inherited Lancashire cotton fortunes from parents and ancestors who had worked and prospered in the 'dark Satanic mills' of the early nineteenth century – a hard-working background which they were a little inclined to forget. Rupert Potter was, in fact, extremely proud of his father, Edmund Potter, not because he was a self-made man – that perhaps least of all – but because he had been Liberal M.P. for Carlisle and a friend of Cobden and Bright, and had died in possession of more money than he knew what to do with. He had been born in Manchester in 1802, into a mercantile family with strong Unitarian convictions and a respect for education. His early life had been hard, but he had had the foresight to go into the calico-printing trade, and – as Trollope wrote of one of his affluent characters – 'made Calico as long as he could get any cotton', to such good effect that in middle-age,

Kensington High Street in 1860,
from Old and New London by Edward Walford

Walking dresses, 1870, from The Milliner and Dressmaker

owner of the Dinting Vale Works at Glossop and a magistrate, he had
found himself at the head of the new industry. He was now, at the time
of his grand-daughter's birth, living in comfortable retirement at Camfield Place in Hertfordshire (all the Lancashire cotton fortunes tended
to move south as soon as they could, for the sake of a kinder climate and
of being landed gentry), and it was this unbeautiful yellow-brick country house which was the background of Beatrix Potter's fondest early
memories. Some of these, she claimed, went back as far as one and two
years old, particularly of 'lying in a crib in the nursery bedroom under
the tyranny of a cross old nurse . . . I can feel the diamond pattern of
that old yellow crib printed against my cheek, as I lay with my head

where my heels should be, staring backwards over my eyebrows at the plaster heads on the chimney-piece.' When she was old enough to sit up to table it was the delicious nursery teas that, especially to a London child, were specially memorable. 'I hope I am not by nature greedy', she wrote many years later, 'but there was something rapturous . . . in the unlimited supply of new milk . . . How I watched at the window for the little farm-boy, staggering along the carriage-drive with the cans! . . . Then we had eggs, so new that the most perverse kitchen-maid could not hard-boil them', and coarse home-made bread with floury crust which was a joy to bite because 'in those days we had teeth'. For many years Camfield remained for her 'the place I love best in the world . . . the notes of the stable clock and the all-pervading smell of new-mown hay, the distant sounds of the farmyard, the feeling of plenty, well-assured, indolent wealth, honourably earned and wisely spent, charity without ostentation, opulence without pride . . .'

It was certainly very different from Bolton Gardens. There, the ticking of the grandfather clock could be heard all over the house, and at the same hour every morning Mr and Mrs Rupert Potter came down to the dining-room for breakfast, a meal consumed in silence. Between ten and eleven Mr Potter left, sometimes for his chambers in Lincoln's Inn, more often for his club. At one o'clock a tray furnished with a small cutlet and a helping of rice pudding went up to the nursery by

Camfield Place, Essendon (detail). Artist unknown

Old Brompton Road, Kensington, the shopping-centre for Bolton Gardens, c. 1900. One side of the Potter house in Bolton Gardens faced a section of Old Brompton Road

the back stairs, and as the clock struck two the carriage was at the door and Mrs Potter, small and inflexibly upright and dressed in black, came down the whitened steps and got into it, and was driven away to pay calls and leave cards on a carefully restricted circle of acquaintance. At six o'clock Mr Cox, the butler, could be observed through the dining-room windows preparing a solemn ritual with napkins and spoons and forks on the mahogany table. Soon the curtains would be drawn and the nursery lamp extinguished, and to the street the house would give no further evidence of life.

There was, however, quite a population below stairs in all the Bolton Gardens houses, behaving well on the whole and causing little disturbance to the residents. Mr Potter employed five – Mr Cox the butler, a cook, two housemaids and a nurse, besides the coachman who lived with his family in the mews, looking after the carriage and horses. The house next door could boast of no fewer than nine servants, and indeed, in the world into which Beatrix Potter was born one of the main problems of family life was finding something to do.

Rupert Potter was a professional man; he had been called to the Bar, and is listed in contemporary Post Office directories as a barrister and solicitor specializing in equity drafting and conveyancing. Certainly he kept chambers in Lincoln's Inn for a good many years and seems to have had some connection with Lancaster Chancery Court as well, but, mysteriously, no evidence has come to light of any practice, and a story was current among the younger members of his family that the only brief he ever received was a hoax – a discovery which he made with great relief. At all events, he had plenty of time on his hands and plenty of money, and although there was a certain dignity in being a barrister, to renounce most of the toil of the profession was perhaps even more becoming in a gentleman. So, while Mrs Potter occupied herself with embroidery, Mr Potter made a life for himself and lived it punctually. He spent much time at the Athenaeum and Reform Clubs, where he read the newspapers; he paid afternoon visits to the studio of John Everett Millais, who lived in Cromwell Place, and he came out strongly as an amateur photographer.

Mr Potter had always been interested in art, spending much of his leisure in visiting exhibitions, particularly at the Royal Academy; he

This photograph by Rupert Potter shows the side entrance of 2 Bolton Gardens, now demolished. This is where the original Mrs Tiggy-winkle was buried.

sketched and drew a little himself, patiently copying engravings and drawings from books and albums; but it was the development of the dry-plate process in photography (which did away with the necessity for a portable dark-room) that brought a creative interest into his life. Like his exact contemporary, Lewis Carroll, he rarely moved without quantities of heavy photographic equipment – large cameras draped in black velvet, special lenses and filters, tripods, cases of glass plates and mysterious chemicals. With these, he gradually achieved a high level of excellence as a photographer. He took views of Scottish scenery, he photographed trees, he arranged serious groups on the steps of country houses, he made portrait studies of Mrs Potter (who often received compliments on her likeness to Queen Victoria) pausing to reflect against a background of conifers, or resting her gloved hand on a rustic post. More interesting still, he took his apparatus on certain afternoons to Mr Millais' studio, and photographed the artist's sitters in the pose in which they were being painted, or supplied scenes which he had photographed himself to be used as background, thus combining the pleasures of his hobby with performing a useful service for his friend. ('Mr Millais', Beatrix wrote, 'says the professionals aren't fit to hold a candle to Papa.') In this way he made an interesting collection of portraits, of which his study of Gladstone – eagle-eyed, a trifle absurd – is probably the best, and is unlikely to have diminished Mr Potter's intense conservative dislike of 'the old person'. (He once refused to raise his hat to him in Bond Street.) There is a family tradition that Millais offered, in return, to paint the rosy little girl he had caught a glimpse of on one of his occasional visits to Bolton Gardens. Beatrix's cousin Kate Potter, a remarkably beautiful child, had sat to Riviere for a charming sentimental nursery picture called 'Cupboard Love', but Mr Potter is said to have refused to have Beatrix painted because it might make her vain.

Beatrix Potter's London childhood was, by ordinary standards, abnormally secluded and lonely. She neither shared her parents' life nor mixed with other children. She was five years old when her brother Bertram was born, and as soon as he was old enough he was packed off to school at Eastbourne, so that apart from a nurse or a visiting governess she was as solitary as before. Yet, if abnormally shy, she was not unhappy; she did not mind being alone; nothing had ever happened to make her afraid of it. She was, besides, able to concentrate on her own fantasies and interests – animals, copying, drawing, every aspect of natural history – with an intensity that would have been impossible in a more companionable life. 'Thank goodness,' she wrote in middle-age, 'my education was neglected; I was never sent to school . . . The reason I am glad I did not go to school – it would have rubbed off some of the originality (if I had not died of shyness or been killed with over-pressure). I fancy I could have been taught anything if I had been caught young; but it was in the days when parents kept governesses, and only boys went to school in most families.'

There was one source, however, of prolonged and recurring happiness for which her parents were certainly responsible. Mr and Mrs Potter spent several months of every year in rented country houses as

Beatrix Potter's dolls

Rupert Potter with John Bright on a fishing holiday in the Lakes

far away as possible from Bolton Gardens ('my unloved birthplace', as Beatrix described it in old age when she heard the house had been destroyed by bombs in 1940), taking the servants and carriage and horses to Scotland by train and inviting one or two serious male friends to share Mr Potter's interest in fly fishing. Perhaps it was the influence of Millais, or his example, which led them for twelve consecutive summers in the 'seventies and 'eighties to rent Dalguise House, near Dunkeld on the River Tay in Perthshire, for Millais was a passionate sportsman when he was not painting, and was often to be found

Sir John Millais and Lily Langtry,
photographed at Eastwood, Dunkeld, by Rupert Potter

with rod and gun in the Dunkeld area, which gave him the romantic background of many of his landscapes. This was a splendid opportunity for Mr Potter as pioneer photographer; he could photograph not only Millais and his wife in country surroundings, but also such celebrities as Lily Langtry when they came to visit. He had, besides, his own fishing guests as subjects; William Gaskell, whose fascinating wife had died some years before, and whom Mr Potter knew through the Manchester Unitarian connection; John Bright, the Quaker orator and statesman, who had been his father's friend and was also a passionate fisherman, though he considered it improper to cast a fly on Sundays. On those pious afternoons he took Beatrix and Bertram for long exploratory walks and recited poetry.

The romantic Scottish scenery, the woods and glens, the roe-deer browsing peacefully in the heather made for the child Beatrix such a visionary landscape of happiness that in after years she was afraid to visit it again. 'I was a child then, I had no idea what the world would be like . . . Everything was romantic in my imagination . . . I remember every stone, every tree, the scent of the heather . . . the murmuring of the wind through the fir trees. Even when the thunder growled in the

A page from a sketch book inscribed '1875 Dalguise'
when Beatrix was eight years old

distance, and the wind swept up the valley in fearful gusts, oh, it was always beautiful, home sweet home, I knew nothing of trouble then.' So peaceful were the long summers at Dalguise, in spite of the appearance of a single railway track connecting Dunkeld with Perth, that Beatrix remembered 'a partridge's nest with an incredible number of eggs in the hollow between two sleepers in the goods siding at Dalguise, where trucks were constantly shunted over the bird's head.' Even the deer were not disturbed by an occasional slow goods train rumbling by – 'they lift their heads and then go on feeding'.

These magical summers at Dalguise continued for twelve years, until Beatrix Potter was seventeen and the house had perhaps been sold, since it was no longer available. By this time her brother Bertram was twelve years old and participating with the utmost seriousness in his sister's nature study and experiments. They decided to make a collection of all the plants, animals and insects they could find, and smuggled home innumerable beetles, toadstools, dead birds, hedgehogs, caterpillars, minnows and sloughed snakeskins. If the dead specimen were not past skinning, they skinned it; if it were, they busily boiled it

A page from a sketch book dated 1876

(opposite below) Notes on
caterpillars written by Beatrix
in a drawing book at the
age of eight
(opposite above) Two pages from
a booklet written by Bertram at the
age of eight or nine

(left and above) Beatrix and Bertram,
photographs almost certainly taken
by their father

and kept the bones. They even, on one occasion, having obtained a
dead fox from heaven knows where, skinned and boiled it successfully
in secret and articulated the skeleton. Everything that they brought
home, they drew and painted. They sewed together little drawing
books out of odd sheets of paper and filled them with drawings of birds'
eggs, flowers, and butterflies. From babyhood Beatrix had had a passion
for paint-box and pencil, and her earliest drawings had nearly all been
of animals and birds, copied from plates in old-fashioned natural his-
tories – kingfishers, eagles, humming-birds, hippopotamuses, things
she had never seen. Now the little books were filled with rabbits, cows,

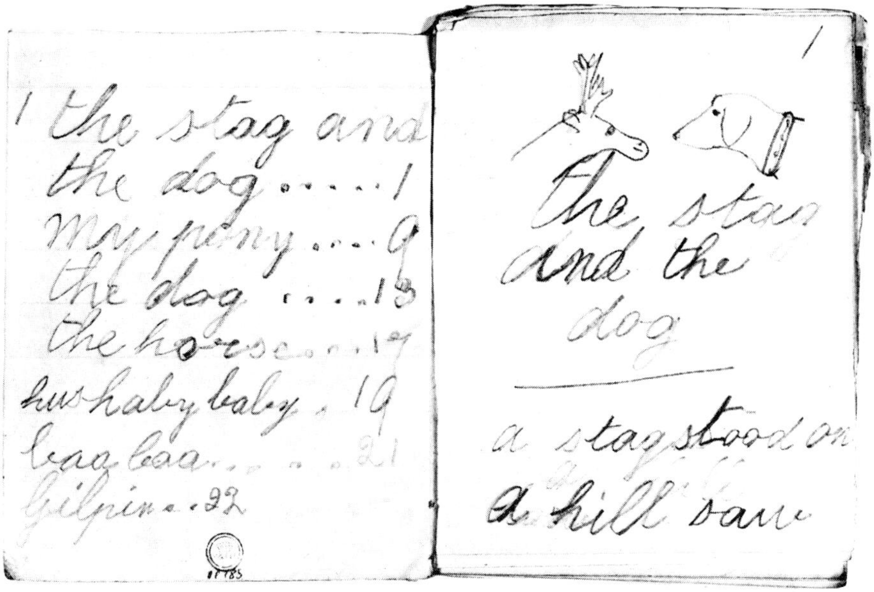

the stag
and the
dog
_____

a stag stood on
a hill one

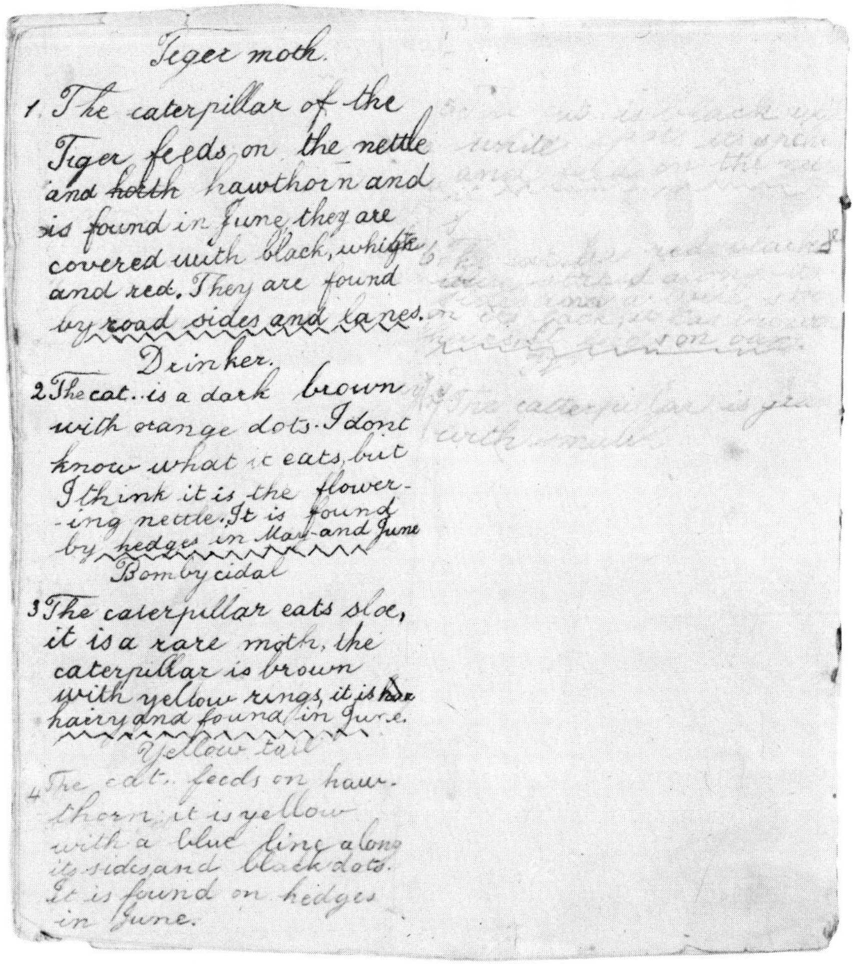

Tiger moth.

1. The caterpillar of the
Tiger feeds on the nettle
and both hawthorn and
is found in June they are
covered with black, white
and red. They are found
by road sides and lanes.

Drinker.

2. The cat.. is a dark brown
with orange dots. I dont
know what it eats, but
I think it is the flower-
-ing nettle. It is found
by hedges in May and June

Bombycidal

3. The caterpillar eats sloe,
it is a rare moth, the
caterpillar is brown
with yellow rings, it is
hairy and found in June.

Yellow tail

4. The cat.. feeds on hawthorn, it is yellow
with a blue line along
its sides and black dots.
It is found on hedges
in June.

sheep, caterpillars, cottages, a leaf or two, a sprig of wallflower, a view
of a dairy. Realistic enough for the most part, and as careful of detail
as a child naturalist of ten years old can be; but here and there on the
grubby pages fantasy breaks through – mufflers appear round the necks
of newts, rabbits walk upright, skate on ice, carry umbrellas, walk out
in bonnets and mantles like Mrs Potter's.

(above) Still life by Beatrix of shells, antlers and
a Japanese calendar. Watercolour drawing c. 1882
(opposite) Study of a pollard willow inscribed 'May 82'

The two of them not only drew every natural object they could lay
their hands on, they discovered an obsolete printing press, 'a hand press
with an agonising squeak', and made elementary wood and lino cuts.
The press had been joyfully stumbled on in a lumber room, complete,
more or less, but without ink. They made their own from soot and
colza oil – 'a sticky black mess, always either too thick or too thin,
mixed on a board and applied to the type with a small roller . . . I can
hear it squeak, and always the type wrenched sideways.' In the hope of
obtaining grown-up sanction for the printing business they proffered a
few labels for jam-pots; but 'the ink was so messy it was confiscated'.

Beatrix at the doorway of 2 Bolton Gardens,
photographed by her father

Since live animals were even more enthralling than dead specimens the two of them developed a passion for collecting and studying wild creatures; and the animals themselves, tolerated up to a point by the Potter parents but sometimes harboured in secret, supplied a kind of intimate companionship which even in their adult years neither Beatrix nor her brother could do without. Rabbits and hares were easily domesticated, soon growing used to dozing on the nursery hearthrug. Bats could be kept in a parrot cage, rats or mice in a wired box. Bertram decided to specialize in birds, and on occasion complicated the family journeys with a jay ('crammed into a little box, kicking and swearing'), an owl or a kestrel. Beatrix had lizards, newts, toads, a tailless robin bought from a street vendor and later compassionately set free. All of these creatures would be transported or smuggled into Bolton Gardens when Bertram went back to school and Beatrix returned to her top-floor life, enlivened only by her miniature zoo, the visits of various governesses and a few drawing lessons. Her remaining dolls, it is true, kept her silent company, but they belonged to the past.

It sounds a suffocatingly boring life for a girl in her teens, but if it had not been so Beatrix Potter's creative urge might have found less opportunity to develop. She had a thirst for creative experiment, for imaginative exercise, which the quiet and solitude of that upper floor encouraged. She read, drew, painted, studied insects through Bertram's microscope, set about the formidable task of learning whole plays of Shakespeare by heart, and also – the strangest and most complex experiment of all – invented a secret code-writing in which she could discreetly record her thoughts, her experiences, scraps of Papa's conversation or the political news that so often put him out of temper.

This extraordinary document, more than 200,000 words written in secret from the age of fifteen until she was past thirty, tells us a great deal about her everyday life, but about her inner experience, her private thoughts, her feelings, very little. About what really went on in her head and heart in those early years Beatrix Potter was as quiet as the tame mouse washing its whiskers in her sleeve, or the hedgehog curled up behind the coal-scuttle.

2

THE YOUNG NATURALIST

It is impossible to know precisely how old Beatrix Potter was when she invented her secret code and embarked on the task of keeping a private journal, since what has survived is not the whole of it. I myself have handled pages transcribed in her own normal hand, of which the cryptic original has never come to light, and there is no knowing how much more may have been lost before the discovery after her death, by her cousin Mrs Stephanie Duke, of that mysterious drawerful of papers at Castle Cottage, Sawrey.

It seems fairly certain, however, that she was between fourteen and fifteen years old when she began keeping her vast journal, written in a cipher which she had evidently invented and perfected some time before, since from the beginning it appears to have been written with speed and accuracy. It is not difficult for an intelligent child to invent such a code, though it can be maddeningly difficult for anyone else to interpret. The system depends mainly on the substitution of one letter of the alphabet for another – B for A or K for B and so on, with the addition perhaps of a few eccentric characters resembling German script or the Greek alphabet. Once this substitution has been learned by heart the code can be rapidly written and all sorts of private matter recorded without fear of detection.

Why this particular child should have felt the need for protective secrecy is of course another matter, though I doubt the necessity of plumbing any great psychological depths to discover the answer. Secrets are irresistibly attractive to most children, and once she had discovered that 'that common person, Mr Pepys', had written his diary in cipher-shorthand she set herself the absorbing task of inventing her own. 'No-one will read this', she wrote with confidence, venturing a severe criticism of one of Michelangelo's paintings. There was the added attraction, too, of knowing that no grown-up could read what she had written. The Brontë children some fifty years before, writing their miniature books in so small a hand that no adult was likely to decipher them, had enjoyed a similar secret satisfaction.

There was another reason, however, which made the project both attractive and absorbing. From quite an early age Beatrix Potter had been conscious of a creative urge which she had been at a loss to know how best to satisfy. Painting every object or creature that struck her fancy – an old barn, a lizard, a bat – was not enough; collecting and classifying fossils or articulating the skeletons of mice was not enough, either; learning the psalms by heart or even composing hymns failed to satisfy the restless energy which demanded that she must also *write*, in spite of the fact that she seemed to have no material. The invention of the code was a challenge to which she responded with zest, recording anything and everything which happened to catch her attention, from 'They are cutting down those big trees along the road' to fragments of Grandmama's conversation. She seems to have embarked on this secret labour of many years almost in spite of herself, driven by an inner command to use her faculties, to stretch her mind, to let nothing of significance escape, to create *something*. In the last few weeks of her life, when

Code-writing from The Journal

Beatrix, aged seventeen, with two friends,
possibly the Martineau sisters

perhaps she had been turning over the jumble of papers in her wardrobe drawer, she wrote to her favourite cousin, Caroline Clark, 'When I was young I already had the itch to write, without having any material to write about . . . I used to write long-winded descriptions, hymns(!) and records of conversations in a kind of cipher-shorthand which I am now unable to read even with a magnifying glass.' Thanks to Leslie Linder's patient labour the magnifying glass is no longer necessary, and this curious document, strangely impersonal for the most part, guarded and secret even under the disguise of code, plots for us the slow course from Beatrix Potter's imaginative beginnings to her unique achievement.

Though the journal, for secretive reasons, was kept out of sight, there was no need to conceal her almost obsessive commitment to drawing and painting. 'It is all the same', she wrote in her private cipher, 'drawing, painting, modelling, the irresistible desire to copy any beautiful object which strikes the eye. Why cannot one be content to look at it? I cannot rest, I *must* draw, however poor the result.' In this pursuit, at least, she derived some sympathetic encouragement from her parents, for Rupert Potter, though by now he had given up drawing for photography, still maintained an inquisitive interest in art, and even Mrs Potter did a little ladylike sketching during the holidays. More encouraging still was the casual but kindly interest expressed by Millais when he glanced at her childish work. 'Plenty of people can draw', he had told her, 'but you and my son John have observation'. His son, Beatrix privately recorded, 'at that date couldn't draw at all, but I know exactly what he meant.' Millais' approval, perhaps, was all the more important because as a child she had been so much afraid of him. He had once, turning her round to the light and studying her face with the dispassionate eye of a painter, observed that it was spoiled by the length of her nose and upper lip. It had also amused him to make her blush, for as a child she had had a brilliant colour 'which he used to provoke on purpose'. But she remembered his encouragement with gratitude,

An early watercolour by
Helen Leech (Beatrix's mother)

*Looking towards the Natural History Museum from an upstairs window
of 2 Bolton Gardens. Watercolour by Beatrix Potter, dated 1882*

having that rare kind of commonsense temperament which is more or
less impervious to vanity.

In her governesses, who also encouraged her devotion to paintbox
and pencil, Beatrix was on the whole fortunate. For the first, Miss Hammond, a woman of gentle manners and considerable intelligence, she
developed a lasting affection. Miss Hammond taught general subjects,
including geography and map-drawing, but left by the time Beatrix
was fifteen, protesting that she could teach her nothing more. After
that there was Miss Carter, who came on certain days to teach German
and French but gave up after two years when she was about to be married. (Some twelve years later it was to amuse the children of that
marriage that Beatrix set off on the trail of Peter Rabbit.) And there
was a Miss Cameron, a teacher of drawing and painting who was engaged for several years at some expense and was not an unqualified

success. 'I have great reason to be grateful to her', Beatrix privately recorded when the lessons ended, 'though we were not on particularly good terms . . . Painting is an awkward thing to teach except the details of the medium. If you and your master are determined to look at nature and art in two different directions you are sure to stick.'

The end of the governess era brought benefit rather than loss, for by a happy chance the Potters had settled in a London area where it was possible for a young person interested in natural history to continue self-education without interference. Only a few minutes' walk from Bolton Gardens, in the Cromwell Road, a vast museum project had been going forward for a number of years and now, in the early 'eighties, was nearing completion. (One of the towers could even be seen from the top-floor windows of Bolton Gardens, and had been made the central point of one of Beatrix's watercolours.) The South Kensington Museum, as the Victoria and Albert was called in its early days, had been opened in 1857 by Queen Victoria and the Prince Consort, and was still in the process of development. It was rather a jumble of buildings, to be sure, with flowerbeds bordering the gravelled approach and a strange multi-domed structure known as the 'Brompton Boilers' serving as a façade, but it already contained many departments of art and science and was well staffed with keepers and curators. Nor

The South Kensington Museum in August 1872.
Watercolour by Charles E. Emery

(opposite) *The Consort Court in the South Kensington Museum.*
Drawing by John Watkins, c. 1875

(below) *The South Kensington Museum in 1863.*
Watercolour by J. C. Lanchenick showing the entrance to the Museum
and the structure known as the 'Brompton Boilers'

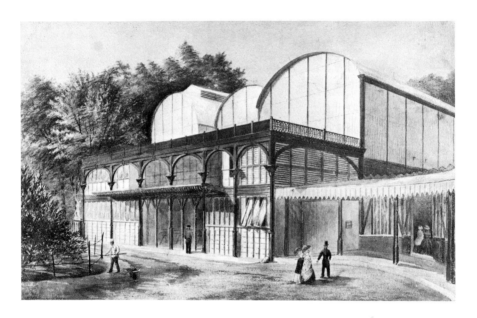

was this all. Next door, so to speak, to this museum of industrial art,
and on a spacious site which until the 'seventies had been mainly occupied by solitary houses and horticultural gardens, the new British
Museum of Natural History had recently been opened, to house the
vast departments of zoology and entomology which were causing increasing congestion in the parent-museum in Bloomsbury.

Afternoon visits to these museums with Miss Hammond or Miss
Carter, or, earlier still, with her nurse or one of the housemaids, had
been one of the few pleasures of Beatrix's London life, as it had been
also of Rudyard Kipling's in the same period, when he and his sister
had been farmed out 'in a tiny lodging-house in the semi-rural Brompton Road.' They, it seems, had gone to the museums unattended – 'No
need in those days to caution us against the traffic' – and now that
Beatrix had reached the age of wearing long dresses with a bustle and
on Sundays a gold watch and chain, no objection was made to her

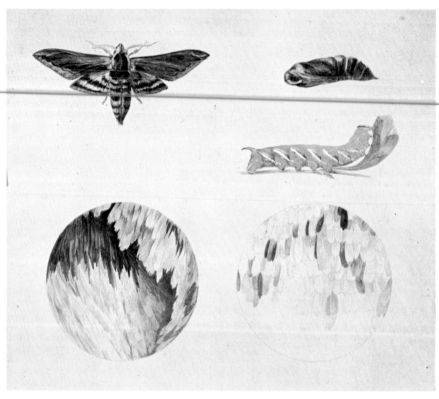

(*above*) *Drawing by Beatrix Potter of a Privet Hawk Moth,*
with caterpillar, chrysalid and magnified sections of the wings, 1887
(*below*) *Drawing of a magnified water-flea, 1887*

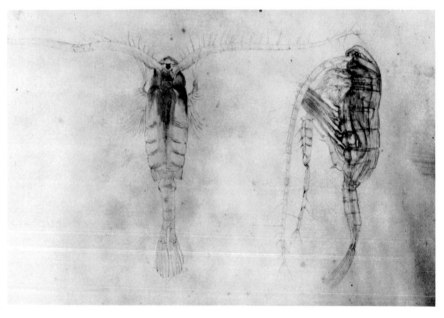

going to the museum alone, to spend long hours leaning over the glass cases with her sketch book, or trying to screw up her courage to ask a question. Even in her thirtieth year, being still as shy as when she was in the nursery, it was an agony to have to approach the museum staff for even a crumb of information. 'Studying labels on insects', she wrote crossly in her journal in 1896, 'being in want of advice, and not in a good temper, I worked into indignation about that august institution. It is the quietest place I know, and the most awkward. They have reached such a pitch of propriety that one cannot ask the simplest question.' In the art museum the atmosphere was easier. 'If I want to find out anything at the library there is not the slightest difficulty, just pay sixpence and have done with it'. But at the Natural History Museum 'the clerks seem to be all gentlemen and one must not speak to them. If people are forward I can manage them, but if they take the line of being shocked it is perfectly awful to a shy person.' When, a few months later, the museum was opened to the public on Sundays, the gentlemanly clerks were absent, and since there was no crowd she was able to spend a pleasanter afternoon. 'Perhaps', she reflected, 'one has more assurance in Sunday clothes and a bonnet?'

Beatrix Potter was probably right in believing that she could have been taught anything if she had been 'caught young'. During those long quiet afternoons in the Natural History Museum (wonderfully, almost intimidatingly quiet in those days – no noisy hordes of schoolchildren, no conducted tours) her fascinated observation led her further and further in scientific directions which, given some encouragement, might have captured her for life. Entomology was endlessly entrancing; now that she saw how specimens were mounted and microscopic plates prepared she could hardly wait to get back to Bertram's microscope, to count the hairs on a caterpillar, copy in watercolour the pseudo-feathery plumage on a hawk–moth's wing, or count the improbable number of whiskers on a bloated tick. Undoubtedly she could have been a happy entomologist, had it not been for the necessity of qualifications, and the superior airs of the experts in the museum offices.

Then again, what about botany? Or, come to that, geology or palaeontology? She could at least boast that by the age of fifteen (perhaps steered through the tests by the knowledgeable Miss Cameron) she had been issued an Art Student's Certificate – whatever that may have meant at the time – and was stated to be satisfactory in model and freehand drawing, practical geometry and linear perspective. The painting of flowers had long been an obsessive occupation, and now that she knew how to make her own dissecting needles and to draw with her eye to the microscope she could pursue the mysteries of pollination and construct theories about the proliferating lichens that had intrigued her during the holidays at Dalguise. The rocks and quarries she had explored during those summer months, collecting specimens in her tin case while Bertram fished, had offered, besides, treasures other than botanical, and she had become obsessed with fossils. 'I have found out which stones to split and how to use a cold chisel . . . Beyond the great oak trees were two large quarries, where I found many fossils, corals, encrinites and a few shells . . .' And a visit to her Hutton cousins at Stroud had introduced her to a dignified old gentleman in a white waistcoat who, being himself an amateur geologist, had popped specimens into his mouth before placing them for her inspection under a magnifying glass. 'He seems to think it positively improper to collect fossils all over the country, but I do not feel under any obligation to confine my attention to a particular formation, viz., the various zones of the Inferior Oölite at Stroud, which I visit once a year for ten days. I beg to state I intend to pick up everything I find which is not too heavy.'

The scientific path which she followed with most determination, however, was mycological. Fungi had become even more fascinating than fossils, and her observations and experiments led even to a genuine discovery and the writing of a learned paper on *The Germination of the Spores of Agaricineae* for the Linnaean Society. The story of this improbable adventure is both touching and absurd. Beatrix Potter by this time was approaching her thirtieth birthday, still leading the enclosed and largely solitary life that had hardly changed in fifteen years. Her health had deteriorated after a bout of rheumatic fever in her early twenties, which was said to have affected her heart. It is equally likely, however, that her 'odious fits of low spirits', her nervous headaches and tendency to feel faint or sick on journeys (symptoms which Mrs Potter was fond of stressing as reasons why Beatrix should never go anywhere alone) were the result of loneliness, boredom and frustration. Sleepless nights, now more than ever, were spent in learning the plays of Shakespeare by heart, the days devoted to as much painstaking work and experiment as could be crammed into them. In 1894 she even became

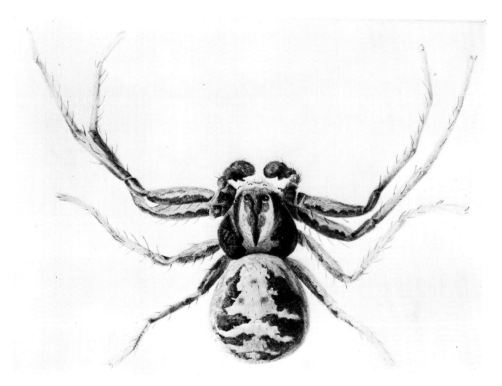

Microscopic study of a male crab spider, 1887

Microscopic study of a tick

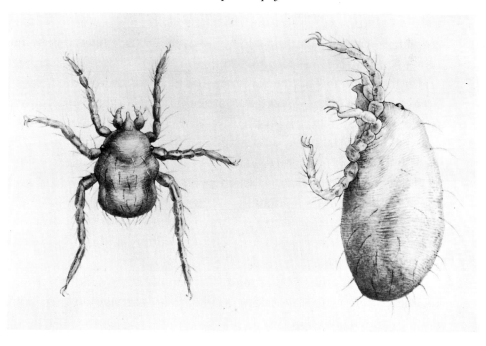

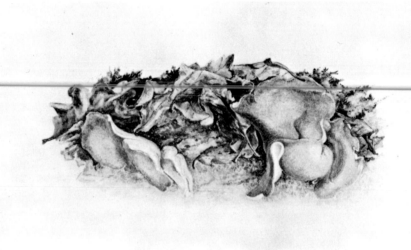

Peziza Aurantia, *found in the woods of Strathallan, October 1893:*
one of Beatrix Potter's many studies of fungi painted about this time

confused about her age. 'It suddenly occurred to me', she wrote – in
code, naturally – 'that I was twenty-eight, not twenty-nine yesterday.
A good deal of geology and Shakespeare might be stuffed into the
extra year.'

It was fungus–hunting, however, which provided her greatest comfort, and only those who have never experienced the pleasure of
amateur botanizing will smile at this new obsession. It was a sport, an
exciting study, which at the same time gave her the material for some
of her best watercolour painting, studies that were scientifically correct
and at the same time aesthetically satisfying. It was during the Scottish
holidays that she first developed this enthusiasm, finding by chance a
fellow addict in the local postman, a 'learned but extremely shy man'
called Charlie Macintosh, whose studies of mosses and fungi can still be
seen, apparently, in the Perth Museum. 'He was certainly pleased with
my drawings', she wrote in her journal, 'and his judgement, speak-
ing to their accuracy in minute botanical points, gave me infinitely
more pleasure than that of critics who assume more, and know less, than
poor Charlie. He is a perfect dragon of erudition, and not gardener's
Latin, either.'

The fungus-hunting had brought a certain measure of independence,
for the Potters were now taking a small pony-carriage on their holidays, as well as the family vehicle, and Beatrix had learned to drive,

trotting off to woods and spinneys far beyond walking distance. 'The fungus starred the ground apparently in thousands', she recorded at Lennel near Coldstream in 1894. 'I found upwards of twenty sorts in a few minutes, *Cortinarius* and the handsome *Lactarius deliciosus* being conspicuous, and joy of joys, the spiky *Gomphidius glutinosus*, a round, slimy, purple head among the moss, which I took up carefully with my old cheese-knife, and turning over saw the slimy veil. There is extreme complacency in finding a totally new species for the first time.' Nelly the pony co-operated obligingly on these expeditions, being 'as near perfection as a lass or pony can be. There may not be much style, but commend me to a horse which will stand still, go any distance, face the steepest road and never stumble once the whole season, and take an amusing and intelligent interest in geography.' (This was gratifyingly different from their black carriage-mare, who was 'perfectly quiet in London, but in the country takes intense interest in the most unlikely and commonplace objects such as milestones, and the square

Study of a toadstool, drawn at Newlands, near Keswick, in the late 'nineties

ends of walls. When fresh, her progress is a course of bob-curtseys from side to side of the road.'

It really seemed, when once she was back in London, that the months, even years, she had spent on her fungi might bear fruit. The idea of illustrating a book on the subject seriously took hold of her. She had now made hundreds of beautifully exact drawings, with minute patience identifying and classifying specimens, dissecting, comparing varieties and checking details at the Natural History Museum. But how was she to go about it? Her parents were not at all sympathetic to her fungus experiments, which had lately extended to dry-rot, so that when she had 'perceived a stout elderly joiner removing quantities of dry-rotten wood from the shop-front of Slater the greengrocer' she had been obliged to sneak out 'after dark with a paper bag and a sixpence'. Another sample of dry-rot, nervously acquired, she had buried under a footpath in the garden. 'How I should catch it; my parents are not devoted to the cause of science. I think I will take it out after dark and grow it in the Boltons. I slept badly.'

Help, however, came unexpectedly in 1896 in the person of her uncle, Sir Henry Roscoe, who, being himself a chemist of some distinction (he had been knighted in 1884 for his services to science) was

*'We went out and across Kew Green to the Herbarium,
a fine old red house with wainscotting and a fine staircase. I think it is one
where Fanny Burney dwelt.' Beatrix Potter's* Journal

more sympathetic than her parents to this cherished project. In a 'sudden
fit of kindness' he proposed taking her to Kew, and this, an event almost
tremulously recorded, was the first of a series of meetings with the
Director of the Royal Botanic Gardens and other august botanists. The
question of whether she would be allowed to go with her 'discreet
uncle' was never certain; on one occasion, when 'afraid of being
stopped from going', she 'escaped out of the house soon after eight and
walked up and down Bramham Gardens to the puzzlement of housemaids' until Uncle Harry emerged to take her to the train.

The botanical experts at the Herbarium were sceptical. 'I am exclu-
sively tropical', the Assistant Director told her, waving aside her portfolio of watercolours. They were passed on to another pontiff, 'a slim,

Studies of a dead yellow-hammer, 3 September 1880

timid-looking old gentleman with a large, thin book under his arm, and an appearance of having been dried in blotting-paper under a press', and eventually into the presence of the Director himself, an intimidating person with a 'dry cynical manner, puffing a cigarette, but wide awake and boastful.' He glanced at the drawings, appeared to be surprised at what he saw, and conversed with Uncle Harry about politics. 'He did not address me again, which I mention not with resentment, for I was getting dreadfully tired, but I had once or twice an amusing feeling of being regarded as young.'

The trouble was, as soon unmistakeably appeared, that an amateur was not quite welcome in these precincts. Not only were the watercolours, as the Director with evident pleasure pointed out, lacking the diagrammatic extension of detail necessary for scientific usefulness, but this unknown young woman had conducted independent experiments and developed theories. She even went so far as to have her own ideas about the propagation of the spores of moulds, and to offer a theory that lichens were actually dual organisms, fungi living in close association with algae. (In this, as it later turned out, she was perfectly right, though forestalled in her small discovery by a learned German.) The Assistant Director was sceptical, and said so. The Director, Mr Thiselton-Dyer, after further visits had been paid to the Herbarium,

Study of a dead fawn

wrote a letter to Uncle Harry which was not only 'stupid' (or so Uncle
Harry considered it) but 'rude'. 'Uncle Harry said he was a little rough-
spoken and knew nothing about the subject . . . He would not show
me his letter. I imagine it contained advice that I should be sent to
school before I began to teach other people.' Sir Henry was justifiably
affronted, and 'expressed animosity against the authorities at Kew.' He
would not, he could not, he insisted, let the matter rest. 'Upon my
word, I was afraid the Director would have taken away my ticket.'
(She had been issued a reader's ticket to the Library.) 'I fancy he may
be something of a misogynist, *vide* the girls in the garden who are
obliged to wear knickerbockers; but it is odious to a shy person to be
snubbed as conceited, especially when the shy person happened to be
right, and under the temptation of sauciness.'

The upshot of this 'storm in a tea-kettle', as she considered it, was
that Beatrix was egged on by her uncle to write a paper on the burning
subject of the spores of moulds, which he went over minutely for cor-
rections, and which was finally, at his suggestion, read before the Lin-

naean Society of London. Not, however, by its author; ladies were not allowed to attend meetings. This success was something, certainly, but it was not much. The excitement of several years had ended in disappointment, and though Beatrix for a time continued in her passion for fungi, she knew now that it would lead nowhere. One by one, with reluctance, the treasured folios of watercolours were laid aside. Their tapes, it seemed, would after all be untied only for the interest of an occasional visitor; and who besides Bertram could be expected to understand the beauties of fungus? (It was not until some seventy years later, in 1967 to be exact, that her illustrations inspired an attractive book on British fungi by Dr W. P. K. Findlay, a past President of the British Mycological Society.)

It was all very disappointing, and she could console herself only with the reflection that at Lennel at least she had done 'a good summer's work'. 'The funguses will come up again and the fossils will keep. I hope I may go back again some day when I am an old woman, unless I happen to become a fossil myself, which would save trouble.'

Beatrix Potter, aged twenty-three

3

THE SECRET APPRENTICESHIP

Millais had certainly been right when he remarked on Beatrix Potter's gift of observation, which now that the fungus adventure had ended in anticlimax brought her back with renewed concentration to her study of animals. In this, as usual, Bertram collaborated when he was at home, keeping a jay and a bat in his bedroom – an unlucky coalition for the latter, since 'that horrid old jack jay, being left alone to bathe in a wash-basin, opened the box and destroyed the poor creature' – and complicating his life with dogs, hawks, owls or whatever fur or feather had taken his fancy. But now that Bertram was more or less grown-up he seems to have absented himself from home as much as possible, disappearing to Scotland to stay with friends, his luggage further encumbered with an easel and vast rolls of canvas, since he had finally decided, with his parents' considered permission, to become an artist.

Beatrix returned, as before and uncomplainingly, to the company of animals, sketching her rabbit, her tortoise or one of her hedgehogs, sorting the records and specimens which she and Bertram had amassed over the years. 'Dusting and mending our little bone-cupboards,' she recorded in her journal, 'when that containing the collection of British mice descended bodily upon my head amidst a shower of glass eyes. I caught the skeleton of a favourite dormouse, but six others were broken and mixed. I mended them all up. I thought it a curious instance of the beautifully minute differences and fittings together of the bones . . .'

Her rabbits, Benjamin and Peter, though 'regular vermin', had given her a strong feeling of 'friendship for the race'. 'Rabbits are creatures of warm volatile temperament', she wrote, 'but shallow and absurdly transparent. It is this naturalness . . . that I find so delightful in Mr Benjamin Bunny, though I frankly admit his vulgarity. At one moment amiably sentimental to the verge of silliness, at the next, the upsetting of a jug or tea-cup . . . will convert him into a demon, throwing himself on his back, scratching and spluttering. If I can lay hold of him without being bitten, within half a minute he is licking my hands as though nothing has happened.'

Her second, Peter, was of a more equable character, and with much patience she had been able to teach him a few tricks. 'He really is good at tricks when hungry, in private, jumping (stick, hands, hoop, back and forward), ringing a little bell and drumming on a tambourine.' After his death, only a month after he had been immortalized in the privately printed edition of *The Tale of Peter Rabbit*, she wrote on the fly-leaf of her own copy: 'In affectionate remembrance of poor old Peter Rabbit, who died on the 26th of January 1901 at the end of his 9th year. He was bought, at a very tender age, in the Uxbridge Road, Shepherd's Bush, for the exorbitant sum of 4/6 . . . Whatever the limitations of his intellect or outward shortcomings of his fur, and his ears and toes, his disposition was uniformly amiable and his temper unfailingly sweet. An affectionate companion and a quiet friend.'

At home in Bolton Gardens, or in Scotland during the holidays, there was usually some quiet obscure companion in her room – a toad squatting comfortably on the writing–table, newts in a glass tank among pebbles and weeds, a hedgehog in a flannel-lined box preparing itself for the ritual of hibernation – and her observations of their behaviour were meticulously recorded. As early as 1883, when she was seventeen, she had noticed that the breathing system of newts differed from that of frogs and toads. 'They, like frogs, can remain under the surface for a long time . . . but there is one thing about the breathing which I never noticed in any other – the newt having put out the used–up air, draws in fresh through quick respiration through its nostril . . . It sinks to the bottom till the new supply is exhausted; but the air when used, instead of returning through the nose, collects in the throat, extending it greatly. Then the newt rising to the surface, lets out the air by opening its mouth wide with a snap.'

At Lennel in 1894 her resident toad decided to abscond, but not before she had made several detailed studies. 'Last week I had the misfortune to lose the toad, but trust that he is enjoying himself as nothing was found below. He got off from the first–floor window-sill. I was sorry to lose him as I had had him more than a year and very tame, turning sharply round for food when I put my hand near him.'

Of all her animal observations of this time, however, her account of the hedgehog's hibernation process is perhaps the most remarkable. She had watched her own tame hedgehogs enter and emerge from the trance state so often that she had become convinced that hibernation was not, as was generally supposed, brought about solely by low temperature. 'The hibernating trance is entirely under the animal's own control, and only in a secondary degree dependent on the weather. My tame hedgehog could rouse herself at half an hour's notice at any time, even during severe frost; and conversely she could "go off" at will on a merely wet day in August, or upon the hearthrug in front of a hot fire. I have watched the somewhat ghastly process on several occasions. The first time I saw it I administered brandy, being under the impression that the animal was dying. The trick is done by swallowing the breath . . . The hedgehog composes itself comfortably, usually after a large meal and an evening of extra liveliness. The idea that it is made drowsy by cold weather is altogether wrong. It closes its eyes and holds its breath, occasionally it catches a breath in spite of itself with a sobbing gasp. The process looks difficult and highly uncomfortable; and the animal is very cross if interrupted. Gradually the involuntary gasps come at longer

Beatrix's pet rabbit Peter, inscribed 'Jan. '98'

'Peter'

Studies of hedgehogs' heads, c. 1904

intervals, and the extremities grow cold and the nose becomes quite dry. In less than an hour the cataleptic state is complete. When the hedgehog wants to return to the world the process is reversed; the breathing which has been slow and faint during the trance is quickened tremendously. I think I have counted 120 respirations to the minute. The first visible result of this vigorous consumption of air is a wetness of the hitherto dry nose. The heat reaches the paws last. The waking up is a much slower process than the going off, and the animal is often painfully weak and nervous for several hours.'

This hedgehog was, of course, that same 'very stout short person' who was Beatrix Potter's intimate companion for a number of years, travelling always concealed in a small basket. 'She enjoys going by train, she is always very hungry when she is on a journey.' Nothing, perhaps, is more typical of the curious 'double vision' of Beatrix Potter's imagination than the two kinds of writing inspired by this appealing little creature. On the one hand is the absorbed naturalist, observing, recording, perhaps even discovering minutiae of animal behaviour; on the other, the poetic vision which could translate the fastidiously clean habits of a species into the diligent laundry business of Mrs Tiggy-winkle. Throughout these years, chiefly in her late twenties, we find details recorded which the magic catalyst of communication with children would bring presently to life.

In 1892, for instance, at Birnam in Perthshire, we find her interrupting one of her solitary photographic outings – she had by now been allowed the use of one of her father's cameras which he found too heavy, 'a most inconveniently heavy article which he refuses to use, and which has been breaking my back since I took to that profession' – for a long talk with 'the immortal McDougall', a middle-aged gamekeeper whom the whole family found an inexhaustible source of memorable anecdotes. (Even Mr Potter had been tickled by his attributing the rough weather 'to the passage of the planet Satan over the Equator.') On this occasion 'he told another curious story of a fox which he trapped in a snare. When he came in sight of it, it was sitting up with the wire round its neck, but on his going round behind it with the intention of shooting it, it flopped down "dead". It actually allowed him to open its eyes and mouth with his fingers, pull it about and carry it home in his game-bag, only dropping the disguise when shut up in an empty room.' Could this have been the beginning of her long acquaintance with that master of duplicity, Mr Tod? It sounds uncommonly like him. 'It lived six years in a kennel and fed upon porridge. It was so sly, it had a habit of saving a portion of porridge within reach of his chain, then pretending sleep, and pouncing on the hens, which it took into the kennel, "feathers and all" ' – a ruse that would surely have succeeded with Jemima Puddle-duck.

But how was all this observation and imagination to be turned to account? For years, now, she had been groping to find the direction which would bring her obsessive work to some kind of fruition. 'I *will* do something sooner or later,' she had written in 1883, after a visit to

*Study of a fox with a chain round its neck, probably an early idea for
a possible book,* The Fox and the Grapes

the Royal Academy with Papa, which left her determined to set aside
'more and more time for painting. I thought to have settled down
quietly', she reproached herself, 'but it seems it *can not* be . . . I can't
settle to anything but my painting, I lose my patience over everything
else. There is nothing to be done . . . Oh, *Faith* – Faith . . .' And a few
weeks before, at a winter exhibition of old masters which had included
works by Angelica Kaufmann, there had been a hint of self-encourage-
ment – 'It shows what a woman has done.'

The great problem was to decide on the chosen direction. Mycology,
in spite of her passion for the subject and the perfection of her watercolours, had ended in frustration. Photography was, to a certain degree,
mechanical, and less aesthetically satisfying than Papa apparently found

it. One could photograph specimens, certainly, or attractive back-grounds which were useful in composition, but as an end in itself she found it unrewarding. Painting skulls, insects, spiders with scientific exactitude was an absorbing pastime, but where could it lead her? She had done some meticulous caterpillar studies for a Miss Martineau, daughter of a Unitarian-theologian friend of Mr Potter's, an un-married lady who appears to have had scientific interests and who lived in Gordon Square; but Miss Martineau and her sisters had revealed themselves as 'spinsters . . . dry and acid to a degree', and the connection had not prospered. Her mother's interests, on the other hand, which were not many, held little attraction for Beatrix, however dutifully she may have supported and approved them. Mrs Potter, following her own mother's example, lived largely for her needle – a device which has undoubtedly saved the sanity of more women than any other inven-tion. But Beatrix was not a needlewoman, and the specially-bound

Studies of caterpillars of a Poplar Hawk Moth, a Puss Moth and
a Privet Hawk Moth, probably an original done for the set of lithographic plates
designed for Miss Martineau, 1895

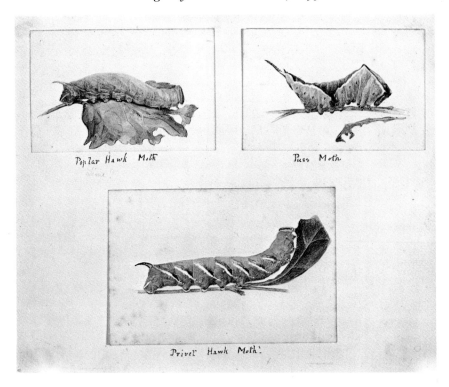

This and the photograph reproduced on the opposite page, both presumably 'set up' by Rupert Potter, show Beatrix's father in two different lights. The group on the steps is one of the relatively rare photographs that show both Beatrix and her brother smiling.

pattern-books of beautiful handmade paper, in which Mrs Potter and
Grandmama Leech before her had sketched out their embroidery designs, were all employed by Beatrix, when late in life she got her hands
on them, as notebooks for roughing out stories and scribbling sketches.
The only occupation of her mother's which seems to have interested
Beatrix at all was her transcribing of books into braille. The process of
stereotyping had not yet been invented, and the letters were laboriously
punched by hand, raising the dots from the back of a sheet of thick
paper. 'Years and years ago', Beatrix wrote in old age, when one of
her own books was being published in braille, 'my mother transcribed
many volumes for a Blind Association in London.' But such charitable
activities, however estimable, offered none of the creative fulfilment
that she yearned for.

Art, only art . . . the absorbing realistic minutiae of Victorian genre
painting, the animal detail of Rosa Bonheur and Landseer, the tender
bucolic vision of Palmer and Constable, these were what fascinated her;
yet here was the inevitable impediment – how could she presume to
think of entering the grandiose world so genially dominated both at
home and at the Academy by Millais? Millais' 'Ophelia', studied and

admired with rapture at the Grosvenor Gallery, was 'probably one of the most marvellous pictures in the world.' In his celebrated 'Bubbles', he used his grandson as his first model and the picture was exhibited at the Royal Academy in 1886. It was soon to be familiar all over the English-speaking world when Pears bought the painting a year later and used it for their soap advertisement. Beatrix had watched it from its beginning as a rough sketch, aided at every stage by Mr Potter's photography. 'Mr Millais came here in the evening,' she breathlessly recorded, 'to get Papa to photograph next morning . . . "I just want you to photograph that little boy of Effie's. I've got him, you know, he's," (cocking up his chin at the ceiling) "he's like this, with a bowl and soap-suds and all that, a pipe . . . he's looking up, and there's a beautiful soap-bubble . . .".' Millais on that occasion had casually asked her how she was getting on with her drawing. 'My certes, I was rather alarmed, but he went to another subject in a second . . .' Millais' genial presence still alarmed her; his was not a world that she could aspire to enter.

By a stroke of good luck, however, the very encouragement she needed was close at hand. When Dalguise House had become unavailable in 1882 the Potters had moved from Scotland to the Lake District,

'Ophelia' by Sir John Millais, 1851–2. Exhibited at the Grosvenor Gallery and described by Beatrix Potter as 'probably one of the most marvellous pictures in the world'.

Sir John Millais' 'Bubbles'. For the pose, Rupert Potter, at Millais' request, took a photograph of the artist's grandson. To complete the picture, Millais used the features of the boy who later became Admiral Sir William James.

renting an ostentatious Victorian-baronial structure called Wray Castle on the shore of Lake Windermere. The vicar of Wray at that time was one Canon Rawnsley, an enthusiast for all sorts of conservationist causes, an authority on the Lake District with more than a score of published books to his credit, a fierce campaigner against all the dangers menacing that lovely and already tripper-infested district. Later, when he removed to the living of Crosthwaite near Keswick, he was to campaign passionately for the formation of a National Trust to buy and preserve places of natural beauty and historic interest for the nation – an ambition which he achieved in 1895, together with Miss Octavia Hill and Sir Robert Hunter; but at the time when he first made the acquaintance of the Potters he seems to have dedicated a certain amount of his formidable energy to encouraging their daughter. Like herself, he was a keen amateur naturalist; like her, too, though more openly, he was a copious writer with a genuine passion for words. He also had what she had not – some knowledge of editors and publishers.

Wray Castle, with the Potter family in the foreground

His suggestions, when he had looked through her portfolios of drawings – not all of them serious natural stuff, for she had experimented with fanciful animal designs for birthday and Christmas cards and one or two trick-pictures to amuse children – were not particularly ambitious, but they were better than nothing. She might, he suggested, illustrate a birthday card or a nursery rhyme for one of those foreign firms like Nister or Hildesheimer & Faulkner, who were making such a success of the new chromo-lithography process recently perfected in Germany. Her brother Bertram was enthusiastic about the idea and they immediately conspired together, having 'decided that I should make a grand effort in the way of Christmas Cards.' Six designs were worked out in secret over the next few weeks, 'taking for my model that charming rascal Benjamin Bouncer', and delivered by Bertram to the firm of Hildesheimer & Faulkner, who, to her delighted astonishment, not only sent her a cheque for £6 but also 'a very civil letter under the misapprehension that I was a gentleman, requiring me to send some more sketches. My first act,' she recorded in her journal, 'was to give Bounce (what an investment that rabbit has been . . .) a cupful of hemp seeds, the consequence being that when I wanted to draw him next morning he was partially intoxicated and wholly unmanageable. Then I retired to bed, and lay awake chuckling till 2 in the morning, and afterwards had an impression that Bunny came to my bedside in a white cotton nightcap and tickled me with his whiskers.'

This was in 1890, when Beatrix was in her middle twenties, and once again it was her Uncle Harry Roscoe who came to her aid, taking her all the way to the City in a fly to make a personal call on the firm of Hildesheimer & Faulkner. Mr Faulkner himself, though civil, was dry and circumspect. 'Not one word did he say in praise of the cards, but he showed a mysterious desire for more.' An uncomfortable feeling developed during the interview that the firm's taste was embarrassingly different from her own. 'He dwelt with peculiar fondness on some terrible cats, or rather little men with cats' heads stuck on their shoulders. His one idea seemed to me to be fiddles and trousers. Now, if there is anything hideous, it is trousers, but I have conceded them in two guinea-pig drawings. He did not strike me as being a person of much taste; in fact he rather gave me to understand, when I objected to drawing such and such an animal, that it was the humour that signified, not the likeness.'

(left) *A watercolour done
about 1894 possibly for a calendar
for Hildesheimer & Faulkner*

(right) *Design for a Christmas card
in the form of a coconut,
printed by Hildesheimer & Faulkner
in the 'nineties*

(far left) *The final illustration
in a three-part sequence, drawn in
1894, entitled 'The White Cat'*

(left) *One of a pair of designs
probably done for Hildesheimer
& Faulkner*

Mrs Moore with Joan Moore

Here at least, however, was some sort of an opportunity, and the work would be paid for. ('I wish I was not always short of money.') Probably her first commission was to illustrate some doggerel verses by an energetic Bristol barrister called Frederic Weatherly who was also a prolific versifier (*Roses of Picardy* had been his great success); these Hildesheimer published as *The Happy Pair*, a set of fancy cards at fourpence-halfpenny. There were other rabbit, mouse and cat pictures sketched out as time went on, which all have a slightly unfamiliar look, as though, in spite of the initials H.B.P. in the corner, they had been drawn by someone else. This slight unfamiliarity of style is due partly, perhaps, to Beatrix Potter's own admiration for the work of Randolph

Caldecott, whose nursery pictures hung round the walls of her room at Bolton Gardens. She had always had, she wrote, 'the greatest admiration for his work – a jealous appreciation; for I think that others, whose names are commonly bracketed with his, are not on the same plane at all as artist-illustrators. For instance, Kate Greenaway's pictures are very charming, but compared with Caldecott she could not draw.' It was, no doubt, her passion for Caldecott which makes the Christmas cards look unfamiliar. And there may be a touch, besides, of the influence of the circumspect Mr Faulkner, who maintained 'that it was the humour that signified, not the likeness.'

The association was aesthetically unsatisfactory and before long given up. Instead of hackneyed trade pictures and Christmas cards she was now letting her imagination run in an entirely new direction, to the delight of a fresh and altogether ideal audience. One Sunday in August 1892, staying once more in Scotland for the long summer holidays, Beatrix noted briefly in her journal, 'Wrote picture letters to the little Moores', and then went on to make notes about sparrows and chaffinches and the state of her mother's arm, which had been bruised by a fall. The 'little Moores', of course, were the small children of her one-time governess, Miss Carter – Noël, Eric, Freda and Norah and, as time went on, four others. They lived on the edge of Wandsworth Common, and from time to time, when the carriage and coachman could be spared, Beatrix would take the long drive south over Battersea Bridge, taking a shawl, a discarded silk dress or other comforts for Mrs Moore and the children. When she was too far away she would write them picture letters, following her own taste and imagination, knowing that whatever she wrote and drew would be received with rapturous delight by her small audience.

A little more than a year after that first casual mention of the picture letters, this time staying near Dunkeld in Perthshire, Beatrix began a letter to Noël in a new vein, making up a simple and agreeable story.

> My dear Noël,
>   I don't know what to write to you, so I shall tell you a story about four little rabbits, whose names were Flopsy, Mopsy, Cottontail and Peter . . .

She had no inkling, yet, that the letter was to prove important: still less that she had found the magic door which she could open with her own key.

*Two designs probably
intended for Hildesheimer
& Faulkner
(left) 'A Game of Cards'
(below) Watercolour
inscribed on the back:
'Golden Corn, October 99,
by H. B. Potter'*

4

CHILDREN AS AUDIENCE

In all the best fairy tales there is a magic spell, a secret door, an unexpected gift or wave of the wand that changes everything; so it is tempting to see the energetic little governess, Annie Carter, in the role of the good fairy. Now transformed into Mrs Moore, with a snug house on Wandsworth Common and a rapidly increasing family, she unconsciously supplied the touch which was to divert Beatrix Potter's creative energies into a new channel.

Noël, the eldest of the Moore children, was in bed with some childish ailment when he received the Peter Rabbit letter posted from Perthshire, where the Potters were spending their three months' summer holiday. It was evidently not the first letter Miss Potter had sent him, though it may have been the first story. Noël was five years old at the time, his brother Eric was four and there were two younger sisters and a new baby.

When the carriage was available it was one of Beatrix's greatest pleasures to drive out to Wandsworth, taking frocks for the little girls which had been bought on shopping excursions with Mama at Woollands or the Army and Navy Stores, or with her cage of white mice for the children to play with, letting them run about the floor until it was time to go. She would draw them pictures, as much, it seemed, for her own amusement as theirs, and tell them about the adventures of her own small animals who led such a busy life, always being packed or unpacked for departure or arrival in the endless cycle of the Potters' ritual holidays.

The carriage and coachman were essential, for the long drive was beyond the power of her own pony, who was getting old, but there were many occasions when she was not allowed the vehicle, which was provoking. 'When I want to drive to Wandsworth in the big carriage,' she wrote to little Marjorie Moore, 'my Mama wants to drive the other way', and still, after another four years of this difficulty, she was complaining in her journal of having been 'much provoked because my mother will not order the carriage in the morning or make up her mind,

to drive to Wandsworth in the big carriage, my Mamma wants to drive the other way; and when your Mamma wanted to call at Bolton Gardens at Christmas, I could not ask her to come, because we had influenza in the house. I hope you did not have ~~this~~ a visit

A page from a letter to Marjorie Moore, 26 January 1900

(opposite) Noël (left) and Eric Moore. It was Noël to whom Beatrix Potter wrote the original story-letter about Peter Rabbit

and if I say I should like to go out after lunch I am keeping her in, and if she does not go and I have missed the chance of a long drive, it is provoking.'

So, on these 'provoking' occasions, as when she was out of reach in Perth or Cumberland, she amused herself and the children with lively accounts of anything that had caught her fancy, sketching in little pictures as she went along, her drawing and handwriting equally clear and expressive. The children kept many of these letters, the girls tying them into little bundles with yellow ribbon and the boys preserving theirs between the pages of exercise books; but some were probably worn out with use or lost, and there is no knowing how many stories of rabbits and mice and guinea pigs and squirrels were fed into the little Moores' crowded nursery (eight children in all, with scarcely more than a year between any of them) before the thought occurred to Miss Potter that there were other children in the world who might be as much delighted with the tales as Noël and his brother and sisters. It is extraordinary when one thinks of it, but in fact seven years elapsed between the writing of the Peter Rabbit letter and the thought taking shape in Miss Potter's mind that if by chance Noël had kept it, she might enlarge the story and turn it into a book. Noël, who was now twelve, *had* kept the letter, and at once agreed to lend it to Miss Potter so that she might copy it.

The intervening years, however, were by no means wasted. Although on the surface her life appears much the same as it had always been – solitary, enclosed, committed to a comfortably dull routine – there are evidences here and there in her journal that she was unconsciously gathering the material of which her private vision would eventually make use. The secret journal itself by 1893 shows signs of fatigue and there are long gaps, as though she could no longer be bothered to record every trivial occurrence. In another two years, indeed, it would come to an end, but in the meantime she still found the laborious code-writing worth while, preserving impressions which might otherwise be forgotten. 'A diary, however private,' she wrote, 'brings back distinctly the memory of what in this case seemed like a most pleasant dream' – the 'dream' on this occasion being a visit to cousins in Gloucestershire which she had been allowed to make on her own, and which was to have important consequences, as we shall see.

For the present, though she was now in her late twenties, she was committed to the unvarying pattern of her parents' lives, and from time to time her code-writing betrays a smothered exasperation. 'I should have enjoyed it more without Papa and the flies,' she wrote after her first view of the battlefield of Flodden; and in the same year, after another three months in Scotland which had given her much private pleasure, 'It is somewhat trying to pass a season of enjoyment in the company of persons who are constantly on the outlook for matters of complaint.' Only she and Elizabeth the housemaid, it seems, had managed to enjoy themselves – 'whereof I take to be the moral that Elizabeth and I had better go there some day for a holiday – to lodgings.' For consolation, and to while away the dawn hours when she was usually awake, she returned to her old pastime of learning whole scenes and acts of Shakespeare by heart. 'I also learned four Acts of *Henry VIII* and ought to have learned all, but I can say this for my diligence, that every line was learned in bed. The Fourth Act is associated with the company of a robin who came in at daylight attracted by sleepy flies, and sat on the curtain-pole or the wardrobe, bold and black-eyed. He only once sang . . .' Was this robin the unconscious model whom she was later to introduce into the book version of *Peter Rabbit*, boldly observant on the handle of a spade while Peter overeats himself on radishes? 'Mice were also an amusement and extremely tame, picking

'First he ate some lettuces
and some French beans;
and then he ate some radishes.'
Original watercolour
for The Tale of Peter Rabbit

up crumbs from the table.' The mouse was a creature she was never tired of drawing – her own little tame one, Hunca Munca, or the house-mice whom she never, even to the end of her life, had the heart to discourage if they stole out at night from the wainscot.

These private and childish pleasures, however, occasionally failed, and she gave way to depression. Her mother fell ill for a fortnight and Beatrix dutifully nursed her, sitting up all night – '. . . an odd experience. There is supposed to be some angelic sentiment in tending the sick,' she added wryly, 'but personally I should not associate angels with castor oil and emptying slops.' Her father was frequently 'troubled with the gravel', which did not improve his temper; the pain was relieved only by 'an extraordinary amount of morphia.' 'Must confess to crying after I got home,' she wrote one melancholy November evening, 'my father being as usual deplorable.' There was even a sudden alarm that Papa might winter abroad, with Mrs Potter and daughter in attendance – a suggestion which so alarmed Beatrix that she went secretly to con-sult their family doctor. 'I fretted so wearily that I went privately . . . and had it out with him . . . I told him plainly I thought it was very startling to be told to go abroad for five months of the year. If my father cannot stand the English winter it is a matter to consider, but seriously we could not stand living five months in a hotel . . . I am anxious to do my best, but I really cannot face going abroad with him.'

The idea fortunately was soon abandoned and the Potters continued their circuit of rented country houses and reliable hotels, where even in the late 'nineties and at their luxurious level the beds had to be care-fully examined. 'I sniffed my bedroom on arrival,' Beatrix methodically recorded at Torquay, 'and for a few hours felt a certain grim satis-faction when my forebodings were maintained . . . I did not undress after the first night, but I was obliged to lie on the bed because there were only two chairs and one of them was broken. It is very uncom-fortable to sleep with Keating's powder in the hair.' Even at Lennel House, near Coldstream, which they had rented for the summer, there was a 'discovery of bugs in the back premises, an event which over-shadoweth all things else.' Mr Potter 'groaned intolerably about the untidiness', but for her part Beatrix was inclined to like the place. 'Much amused with tameness of birds, sparrows in dining-room and swallows' nests all round the house.' The owners were 'said to be fond of mice, and a robin was seen stealing butter in the larder.'

Rupert Potter, 1890

Bertram Potter

*Beatrix with her mother and friends
at Holehird, Windermere*

As time went on (she was now approaching her thirtieth birthday) a new element was cautiously allowed into her life. When Bertram was available, which seems to have been rather rarely, it was accepted that brother and sister might make occasional brief excursions on their own, staying in suitable lodgings in country or seaside places where Bertram could fish and paint and Beatrix wander about as she pleased, drawing whatever stirred her imagination and relaying all sorts of amusing details in letters to the little Moores, or to her own first-cousin once removed, Stephanie Hyde-Parker, who was a fairly recent addition to the family circle.

Opposite is a photograph of Beatrix Potter's cousin, Stephanie Hyde-Parker. On the right is a sketch of her by Beatrix

'I am staying in such a funny old cottage,' she wrote to Freda Moore, who had just had her ninth birthday; 'it is like the little mouse-houses I have often drawn in pictures. I am sure (when I am half-asleep) that it is a mouse-house, for Mrs Cooke, the landlady, and her family go to bed up a sort of ladder-staircase, and I can hear them scuffling about upon the rafters just above my head! The ceiling of my bedroom is so low I can touch it with my hand, and there is a little lattice window just the right size for mice to peep out of. Then there are cupboards in the walls, that little people could hide in, and steps up and down into the rooms, and doors in every corner; very draughty!' On this occasion she sketched her bedroom and the cottage parlour in two different styles – one a literal portrayal, with Bertram's kestrel on the back of a chair and Peter Rabbit on the carpet, the other a light-hearted fantasy in Freda's picture-letter, the same rooms inhabited by a mouse family – an early version of *The Tale of Two Bad Mice*.

Interior of dressing-room at Derwent Cottage, Winchelsea, 26 January 1900

How far Beatrix and Bertram confided in one another it is impossible to know, but I suspect they were pretty much in each other's confidence and that Beatrix knew more than her parents did about her brother's frequent absences from home. Not that there was anything improper about his disappearances to Scotland and elsewhere: he was reticent and secretive to a degree, but it seems he was concealing no more than a determination to leave home, to live in the country as far away as possible from his parents, and eventually, since he was now finally disenchanted with his own painting, to be a farmer. This in time he successfully achieved, buying a small farm in Roxburghshire, ostensibly as an investment (as Beatrix herself was to do later, in the village of Sawrey) and disappearing for good into the Border country. Here, in the parish of Ancrum and without breaking the shocking news to his parents, he married a wine merchant's daughter called Mary Scott, whose father kept a shop in Hawick High Street, and, one hopes, lived happily ever after, or at least until the age of forty-six, when he died suddenly of a stroke.

lattice window just the right size for mice to peep out of. Then there are cupboards in the walls, that little people could hide in, and steps up and down into the rooms, and doors in every corner;—very draughty! I wish

Drawings of Derwent Cottage in a letter to Freda Moore

How much Beatrix knew, or guessed, there is no telling. Bertram had always been a bit of an enigma and she had sometimes privately wondered what would become of him. 'I wonder how he will turn out?' she had once speculated in her journal. 'Sometimes I am hopeful, sometimes I am feared. He has an absorbing interest' – his painting, presumably – 'which is a very great help in keeping anyone straight. The best upbringing has sometimes failed in this family, and I am afraid that Bertram has *it* in him. Heaven grant it is not so, but I am afraid sometimes.' What 'it' was, one can only guess; probably, under his quiet manner, a secret determination and self-will. Beatrix, as captive unmarried daughter, had no chance or inclination to compete with her brother in that field, but clearly she enjoyed her brief escapes in his company, sometimes travelling so far and so fast that there was scarcely time to scribble a line to the children. 'I intended to have written to you sooner,' she wrote to eight-year-old Marjorie, 'but I have been travelling about so much I have always been too sleepy . . . My brother and I left Keswick on Tuesday 16th, came through Carlisle to Dumfries,

(opposite) Bertram and Beatrix

(right) Caroline Hutton

then to Kirkcudbright, then to Stranraer and Belfast, back to Stranraer, to Ayr and Dumfries . . . I have seen so much I shall have to pick out things to tell you about.' Some of the things which she and Bertram had seen would later be remembered and woven into her stories.

More stimulating even than these brother–and–sister excursions were those occasions when, at nearly thirty, Beatrix was sometimes allowed to travel alone. She had gone unaccompanied, or with a maid, once or twice to her grandmothers' houses, but at the time of her first visit to her Hutton cousins at Harescombe Grange in Gloucestershire she had 'not been away independently for five years. It was an event.' So much of an event, apparently, that her mother all but succeeded in persuading her not to go, until her cousin Caroline Hutton entered the battle. In old age Mrs Clark of Ulva, as she had become, clearly remembered the argument and struggle. 'I am always glad,' she wrote to me in her eighties, 'that in spite of her mother's objections I managed to get her to my old home. She said B. was so apt to be sick and to faint; and I, regardless of the truth, said I was quite accustomed to all that; and of course she could do most things, quite long walks included.'

Caroline was some three years younger than her third cousin, and held all sorts of radical and free-thinking views which Beatrix found stimulating, if rather outrageous. They talked at night in their dressing-gowns, brushing their hair, and Beatrix decided that Caroline was 'a pickle'. Like an attractive and provocative Shavian heroine she 'talked of labourers, their miserable wages of eleven shillings a week, their

Drawing of mice done for Hildesheimer & Faulkner in 1890 and later published as a Christmas and New Year card

unsanitary cottages, their appalling families and improvidence.' Beatrix took a genuine interest in politics, but was as fierce a Tory as her father, and Caroline's socialist views and outspoken feminism somewhat shook her. Her dismissive attitude towards marriage, Beatrix confided to her journal, was 'the only flaw that I can find in Caroline. Latter-day fate ordains that many women shall be unmarried and self-contained, nor should I personally dream to complain, but I hold an old-fashioned notion that a happy marriage is the crown of a woman's life.'

Caroline's outspoken agnosticism disturbed her less, since in some ways she found herself in sympathy with it, though disapproving her cousin's freedom of speech in the presence of her more conventional mother and sister. For her own part, she wrote in private, 'I think creeds and manners of worship are of the least possible consequence . . . I shall always call myself a Unitarian because of my father and grand-mother, but for the Unitarians as a dissenting body, as I have known them in London, I have no respect. Their creed is apt to be a timid, illogical compromise, and their forms of service a badly performed imitation of the Church . . . We are not Christians in the commonly accepted sense of the term. It is not possible to appreciate religion in other people while oneself disbelieving creeds, and fully alive to the narrowness of rectors' wives and the fatuity of curates.' Of all the dissenting meetings which from time to time she had sampled with her father she found herself inclined to prefer the Quakers. 'There is something in the sentiment of a Quaker meeting so exactly quaint and fine that a very little oversets the balance . . . but to those who can feel the charm . . . it is exquisitely pleasant.' She had once, attending a Friends' Meeting, summed up her feelings in a simple and unconsciously Beatrix Potter manner: 'I liked it very much . . . I thought it so pleasant in the stillness to listen to a robin singing in the copper beech outside the porch. I doubt if his sentiments were religious.'

Caroline's father, Mr Crompton Hutton, a magistrate and relentless interrogator, she found disconcerting, since there was no limit to the scope of his questions. Her sense of humour, however, came to her rescue, for under the magisterial façade and aggressive cross-questioning she perceived 'one of the kindest of old gentlemen, and certainly a character . . . He is not a very active magistrate, it is more a matter of meddling in small things.' He had a passion for harassing gypsies, whom he consigned to Gloucester Jail on the smallest excuse, even going out 'at the edge of dark' if he suspected a furtive caravan in the area. But it was his appearance, perhaps, which chiefly won her affection. When his stout presence had first confronted her he had 'regarded me critically through his spectacles. He had on large gaiters and seemed hungry.' Was her Uncle Hutton, then, the imaginative first glimpse of that amiable but invasive character, Mr Jackson?

The magic spark, however, which instantly focused her imagination on Gloucester came from a story which Caroline told, having heard it from a local lady who had it from a tailor. The man had been working late into the night on a beautiful waistcoat for a special occasion, but not being able to finish it had gone home to bed in a state of great depression. Next morning, to his amazement, he found the waistcoat finished – all but the last buttonhole, which had a scrap of paper pinned to it inscribed in tiny writing – 'No more twist'. How had it been done? No doubt, said Caroline teasingly, it had been done by fairies, in whom Cousin B. had confessed to believing longer than most. Well, that was a possibility, and would make a good subject one day for a picture-letter. But the more she thought about it the more Beatrix found that she preferred mice to fairies, and became so enchanted with the story that she drove into Gloucester with Caroline and made sketches of the old streets around the cathedral and, later, interiors of some Cotswold

cottages with four-poster beds and wooden dressers covered with ancient crockery. Then, at Harescombe Grange itself she persuaded the coachman's little boy to sit cross-legged like a tailor so that she could sketch him, all with a view to making up a special tale for Freda Moore who was always asking for a story.

The queerest thing about this one, as Miss Potter eventually wrote to Freda, was that it was true – 'at least about the tailor, the waistcoat and the "No more twist"!' What had really happened was this. The tailor had been struggling to finish a specially grand waistcoat for the mayor of Gloucester, who would be leading the procession from the Guildhall to the annual agricultural show. He had failed to finish it in time, and had gone home in despair. What he did not know was that his two assistants, wishing to do their master a good turn, were planning to let themselves secretly into the shop at night and stitch away until the job was done – which they achieved all but the last buttonhole, for which there was no more thread. These notes and sketches were

Original watercolour drawing for The Tailor of Gloucester

stored away in her drawing books while she brooded on the story of the tailor after her own fashion.

The following year at Gwaynynog, her Uncle Fred Burton's home in Denbighshire, being enchanted with the low-ceilinged rooms and solid old furniture, she studied and sketched the rooms with loving attention, lingering over the traditional carving of stout Welsh dressers and court cupboards, of elegant high-backed chairs and grandfather clocks, as though she felt some compulsion to record them. The house was, indeed, interesting on several accounts, and to Beatrix particularly so because in 1774 Dr Johnson had stayed there with the Thrales. The house was then the ancestral home of the Myddleton family, who, according to Uncle Fred, 'by a lavish prodigality were reduced to living in the kitchen'. Being notably 'stingy' himself, and 'very mean as to ha'pence' he had 'dwelt upon their dissipation with unction' and liked to think they had suffered for their extravagance. Johnson and the Thrales, nevertheless, had been handsomely entertained. Mrs Thrale,

Memorial urn to Dr Johnson at Gwaynynog

it is true, was inclined to sniff at the company, all 'genuine Welch folks', but admitted in her diary that 'The men, however, were not drunk nor the women inclined to disgrace themselves . . . The dinner was splendid and we had ices in the dessert.'

Their host, Mr John Myddleton himself, was so impressed by having the Great Cham under his roof that he decided to erect an urn in the garden to commemorate the event, a compliment which Johnson thought both unsuitable and absurd. 'Mr Myddleton's erection of an urn,' he wrote to Mrs Thrale, 'looks like an intention to bury me alive . . . Let him think for the present of some more acceptable memorial.' A handsome classical monument, nevertheless, was eventually raised, and one sultry afternoon Beatrix with her cousin Alice and one of the maids made an appropriate pilgrimage to the dell where Johnson (or so Mr Myddleton said) had 'delighted to stand and repeat verses,' and where now the great stone vase gleamed behind iron railings. 'We had a picnic tea down at Dr Johnson's, provided by Polly . . . She made a most excellent treacle-pudding which, combined with the thunder, had disastrous effects upon Alice and me, and finally Polly herself, who took to her bed with two pills and a seidlitz powder.'

It was the walled garden of the old Welsh house, however, which left the most sympathetic impression on Beatrix Potter's memory, being the kind of practical country garden that she loved best – a random but fertile mixture of flowers, fruit and vegetables, with cabbages flourishing beside arches of climbing roses in beds traditionally framed in clipped box borders. 'The garden is very large,' she noted, 'two-thirds surrounded by a red-brick wall with many apricots, and an inner circle of old grey apple-trees on wooden espaliers. It is very productive but not tidy, the prettiest kind of garden, where bright old-fashioned flowers grow amongst the currant bushes.'

It was this beautiful and endearing garden, with its warm brick walls and secluded gardener's cottage, that came back to her with renewed delight some thirteen years later, when she saw the paths and hedges, the stone walls and the ditch where Mr McGregor emptied his lawn-mowings, as the perfect setting for the tale of the Flopsy Bunnies.

5

SAWREY DISCOVERED

For the long summer holiday of 1896 Rupert Potter decided on a large early-Victorian house in Cumbria, standing on rising ground above Esthwaite Water. He and his wife and Beatrix had inspected it in the late spring, travelling north and staying at the Ferry Hotel in Windermere to compare the various available furnished properties.

This one, Lakefield, seemed to offer everything: fishing for Mr Potter, lake and fell country of incomparable beauty, even family connections in the area with whom Mrs Potter could exchange afternoon drives. Their stay was brief and businesslike; Beatrix dismissed it in her journal as 'not eventful'. They had been into Kendal once, on market day, to consult a house agent; she had been interested in the crowds and the hiring-fair for farm servants, but the most notable detail of the visit seems to have been that on the two long railway journeys between London and Windermere she was 'allowed to undertake the luggage'.

The house once checked for cleanliness and decided on, no time was wasted on exploring the little village of Near Sawrey which lay only a few hundred yards away, with its post office and smithy and Tower Bank Arms, and a little slate-roofed farm called Hill Top looking across Esthwaite Water to the Coniston fells, over woods and stone walls and good rich pasture which had not changed in centuries. Two months later, in July, Beatrix would make this private discovery for herself, with that mysterious inner sense of recognition which cannot be explained. ('I have often been laughed at for thinking Esthwaite Water the most beautiful of the Lakes.') The village of Sawrey, with the down-to-earth simple existence that it epitomized, was to be the source of her greatest happiness and creative life.

Existence meanwhile in Bolton Gardens dragged on as before, enlivened only by that obsessive passion for fungi which was to end in disappointment. Apart from her researches at the museum it had been a tedious spring following a depressing winter. Even Christmas, which with true Unitarian spirit the Potters ignored, or observed only on the level of an ordinary Sunday, had been 'not pleasant'. The weather had been wet and dark, Bertram for some private reason had silently sulked, and since the stock market had been shaken by a row between Britain and the United States over a boundary dispute the household had groaned under the 'interminable rule of the sums and stock-broking calculations which would never come right'. Mr Potter had sold his wife's Canadian securities in a panic and now, 'nearly beside himself', was scanning the financial pages in despair. 'My father, always accustomed to get the newspapers on his mind,' was more than usually 'deplorable. Especially bad this morning before going to chapel.' There was nothing to do but retreat upstairs to the nursery, where at least Peter Rabbit was amiable company during the day, and in those wakeful night hours when she confessed to 'feeling very much down', there was the consolation of reading Wordsworth and the Old Testament. 'I also', she wrote privately in code, 'increasingly derive consolation from a less elevated source, the comfort of having money. One must make out some way. It is something to have a little money to spend on books and to look forward to being independent, though forlorn.'

The money, it seems, had come from an unexpected gift bestowed by her father in one of his financial tremors. 'My father gave me rather

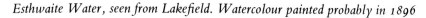

Esthwaite Water, seen from Lakefield. Watercolour painted probably in 1896

an extraordinary present,' she recorded in May, 'viz, certain bonds of the North Pacific Railway which have paid no interest since April '93, the company being in the hands of receivers.' She had 'proceeded into the city with my father in order to make hay with my £5000 . . . The broker advised me to hold on as I was young, but considering I have had the rheumatics, and there was no particular prospect of any interest, I thought I would get out of it.' The bonds sold for £100, which was not very much though obviously better than nothing. ('I did not of course lose on the transaction,' she concluded reasonably, 'because it was a present.')

She was becoming increasingly and stoically aware of her own isolation. 'I wonder why I never seem to know people,' she wrote, brooding on the puzzle. 'It makes one wonder whether one is presentable.' Occasional visits to exhibitions with her father or a convenient aunt produced no personal contact; she would sometimes study the crowd as intently as the pictures, but this only increased the sensation of being an outsider. 'As to the pictures, we saw them splendidly,' she wrote after a private view at the Academy, 'but for the company, unfortunately neither my aunt nor I knew who people were . . . My aunt pointed out one lady and gentleman as the Duke and Duchess of Westminster, which I'm positively certain they weren't. However, there were many pretty dresses and a few sweet faces, and I daresay some (at least) of the haggard gentlemen were Dukes . . . and I judged them all up to my own satisfaction.'

As always, her response to animals was more direct than to people. She had a sharp eye for the horses thronging the streets in those noisy days before the motor-car, and a shopkeeper's sleek well-fed cat was always to be preferred to a reputed duchess. 'The sweetest spectacle I have lately seen,' she wrote after a visit with Mama to the Civil Service Stores (which in those days were in the Haymarket) 'was the Stores' cat, its paws folded under its white chest, its ears and white whiskers laid back, ignoring the roar of the Haymarket, in a new red morocco collar, couchant on a pile of biscuit canisters.'

Wandsworth was still her best resource when the carriage was available, for the Moores were not the only family that could be visited. There was, in fact, a little cluster of elderly cousins, Caroline Hutton's unmarried uncle and aunts, living together in a large old house called Putney Park which still had the air and surroundings of a country

estate, although the borders of its fields, lying between Barnes Common and Putney Heath, were gradually turning into a pleasant suburb.
The house is still there today, only a few minutes' walk from Roe-
hampton village, which for the past fifty years or so it has served as a
social club; but in the 'nineties, when Beatrix Potter knew it, it had
still its own small farm with haystacks, cattle, pigs and poultry, and a
muddy pond with ducks, which she once 'trudged round with Miss
Annie, rather near the bull.' The house itself was 'oddly up and down
and roundabout,' complicated by double doors of a confusing nature.
She had 'never quite mastered the geography of the back passages,
where doors apparently similar let one into closets or the kitchen, or
quite unexpected apartments, with glimpses of people disappearing
through other double doors.' It was a pleasant place to visit, for the
female cousins, especially Miss Annie, were still lively and intelligent,
and could occasionally produce interesting acquaintances, such as the
celebrated Mrs Hugh Blackburn, whose *Birds Drawn from Nature* had
been presented to Beatrix by her parents on her tenth birthday – 'The
book was bound in scarlet with a gilt edge. I danced about the house
with pride.' Now, after twenty years and with her own experience as
a naturalist behind her, she considered that though Mrs Blackburn's
birds 'did not stand on their legs as well as Bewick's . . . he is her only
possible rival.' It had been an impressive experience actually to meet her.

Occasionally, too, children now came to Bolton Gardens for tea –
little cousins of one remove, like Stephanie Hyde-Parker, or the grandchildren of London acquaintances of her mother's. On these occasions
Peter Rabbit would be brought down to the drawing-room and would
mildly exasperate Beatrix by his behaviour. 'Mrs Bruce's children to
tea,' she recorded at the end of a long winter afternoon, 'nice little girls
but very shy. Peter Rabbit was the entertainment, but flatly refused to
perform although he had been black-fasting all day from all but mischief. He caused shrieks of amusement by sitting up in the armchair and
getting on to the tea-table. The children were satisfied, but it is tiresome
that he will never show off.' If he had only stamped his hind-foot that
would have been something, since like all his race Peter was capable of
sounding a tribal alarm of astonishing vigour. 'What a strange thing
force is,' she was musing a few months later, after watching some work-
men sinking a water-pump, 'that a man should bring a thing in a
carpet-bag which is capable of lifting three tons. Force is said to be

Tenby Harbour, 12 April 1900

interminable. I sometimes reflect what may happen when Peter Rabbit stamps, which is one of the most energetic manifestations of insignificance which has come under my notice.'

The sinking of the water-pump had been at Swanage, where in the spring Beatrix and her parents had come for 'an idle fortnight, chequered by toothache', staying at an establishment run by a Miss Vincent under the impressive name of the Royal Victoria Hotel.

('Clean, civil, rather poor for the money, and singularly tough food.')
Papa as usual had been unwell, but on the whole she had 'seen worse
outings' and had managed to spend one solitary afternoon looking for
fossils in the Corfe Castle clay pits and quarries. The only memorable
thing about the visit was that she had seen 'a fine meteor . . . rather
larger and more striking than Jupiter, *white* with a *red* compact trail . . .
I was much impressed by it, a strange visitor from the outside of the
world. I do not often consider the stars . . . it is more than enough that
there should be forty thousand named and classified funguses.'

The family Easter holiday always lasted a fortnight, and was usually
spent at the seaside at Tenby, Sidmouth, Falmouth, Torquay, Wey-
mouth, Lyme Regis or elsewhere along the south coast. Mrs Potter
passed the time in going for drives, while Mr Potter employed himself
in visiting antique shops and sitting on esplanades. 'Very horribly
windy', Beatrix wrote in her journal one April Sunday. 'In the afternoon sauntered about with Papa, and sat a long time on a seat in the
Dorchester Road looking at the Sunday-school children and the little
gardens. Thought rather sadly what a strange thing it was for him to do.'

Whenever she was left to herself, of course, there was no problem.
At Tenby one could hire a boat and be rowed along under the high
cliffs and watch the sea-birds and rabbits. 'I go out every morning,' she
wrote to Marjorie Moore, who was now ten years old and interested
in everything, 'and I generally tell the boatman to row close in under
the cliffs so that I can watch the birds. The rocks are a tremendous
height, as high as a church, and quite straight from top to bottom in
many places, but sometimes there are little ledges halfway up with wild
cabbages growing on them, and at the top where there is soil there is a
row of rabbit holes. What a very funny place for cabbages and rabbits,
right up in the air! My boatman says he has sometimes picked up poor
dead rabbits that have tumbled off; but as long as they don't go too
near the edge – or if they have a little railing – it is a very nice safe place,
for nobody can possibly get near them and their little cabbage gardens.'
This account, as always, was lucidly illustrated with sketches of the
Tenby rabbits and their habitat. It all looked very idyllic, but soon she
discovered that the population had a terrible problem – puffins. 'They
are considered very silly,' she wrote to Freda, Marjorie's next sister,
'and look something like parrots that have tumbled into the water, but
they behave in a very sly way. They never take the trouble to build

nests, but live in rabbit holes. They look for a nice hole and drive the rabbits out. They do not live here in the winter but arrived about a fortnight since; it must be most annoying to the rabbits to see them landing. There are little rabbits by this time, lots of them, all comfortable in bed, I am sure they don't give up their holes without a fight! I don't believe either rabbits or puffins are able to hurt much, but the puffins always win and take possession of the best holes. I don't know what becomes of the rabbits; perhaps they go and live with the jackdaws, who are much more polite; they walk about bobbing their heads as if they were bowing. I notice the rabbits and jackdaws live close together quite nicely.'

At last the day came when the Potter family, including Bertram, travelled up to Sawrey with coach, horses and servants and moved into Lakefield. In no time at all Beatrix was relaying adventures and discoveries to the little Moores. She had been to call on her cousins, the Gaddums, and was soon writing to Eric, 'My little cousin Molly Gaddum has got a squirrel who has two baby squirrels in a hay nest, you cannot think how pretty. They are not much bigger than mice yet. They live in a box in the hay-loft, and one day Molly opened the lid and Mrs

Squirrel jumped out. They had such a business to catch her.' And presently, 'Our coachman brought his cat in a basket. It mewed dreadfully among the luggage, but I think it is enjoying itself. It sings songs with the gardener's cat, which is grey, and the farm cat, which is white with a black tail. There is a very pretty collie dog, it is so clever with the sheep, it drives them right and left, whichever way it is told and never bites them. Sometimes it comes in at our dining-room window and shakes hands.' And finally, reminded of Bertram's inevitable travelling companions, 'We have got a tame owl, he eats mice; he sits with a tail hanging out of his mouth . . .' and so on, scribbling her tiny pen-and-ink pictures on the page as she wrote, unconsciously collecting material and scattering it as soon as she had it among the children at Wandsworth.

At first the weather was wet, 'most tremendous rain', but she and Bertram were in high spirits, exploring the house and poking about among lumber in the attics. 'There are some ancient pistols and an ancient case and velvet hunting-cap. Bertram turned out a portfolio of chalk drawings, figures and heads, in the style of Fuseli, such as young ladies drew at school sixty years since.' Next day the weather improved and they were out with Bertram's dogs across the heath that they called 'our moor', wading through heather and muddy bracken, where they 'came upon a small but very lively viper which we killed with a stick.' They would not have done this, she noted, if they had been wearing gaiters and if the dogs had not run some risk of being bitten. It was all rather like the old days, when they had carried out their nursery experiments. 'We cut off the head which soon ceased to nip, but the tail was obstreperous for an hour and still winced for another hour in the spirit – I hope mechanically! They are exceedingly pretty.'

Her birthday, on 28 July, was 'a perfect, hot summer day', cloudless until late evening, when the weather rolled up like thunder over How Fell. 'I feel much younger at thirty than I did at twenty,' she wrote that night, 'firmer and stronger both in mind and body.' (Sawrey was already beginning to weave its irresistible spell.) The little Gaddum cousins had come to tea and she had walked part of the way home with them and their nursemaid, 'gossipy roly-poly Anne', in the pleasant evening light, helping to push the children in their light mail-cart and delighting to see the 'village people up and down the road and in the flowery little gardens.'

Sawrey offered exactly the life that she had always longed for; not Lakefield itself, that was too much in the formal gentry-image to appeal; it was the grey stone cottages and farmyards, the little front gardens bursting with flowers and vegetables, tidy front-parlours and well scrubbed kitchens, the miraculous skill of the sheepdogs managing their flocks, responding to a light whistle or movement of the hand as though they and the watching shepherd were one person – these were the things that delighted and enthralled her beyond measure, filling her mind with images and incidents to which her whole being responded, and which she would lovingly turn into stories for the little Moores.

Towards the end of their three months' stay in this enchanted area, with Bertram already preparing to disappear to Scotland and the weather becoming stormy, Beatrix with Elizabeth the housemaid drove over to Wray Castle where they had stayed some fourteen years before, to visit the friendly servants they remembered. 'We had a very pleasant time . . . Down in the scullery of the great kitchen Jane had a clothes-basket full of elderberries for wine . . . She had already made damson wine and ginger, and outside was a litter of walnuts blown down by the gale . . . We had a very good tea in the kitchen. I am at a separate table to my amusement, with plates out of the State set, and a sort of cold apple-pastry, something local and heavy.'

The last day was spent in farewells in the village, in packing up her precious fungus collection and saying goodbye to the young farmer and his wife at Hill Top, only a couple of fields away, where she now knew most of the animals by name and every homely detail of the farmhouse. 'I was very sorry to come away, in spite of the broken weather. It is as nearly perfect a little place as I ever lived in, and such nice old-fashioned people in the village . . . Perhaps my most sentimental leave-taking was with Don, the great farm collie. He came up and muddied me as I was packing up Peter Rabbit at the edge of dark. I accompanied him to the stable-gate, where he turned, holding it open with his side, and gravely shook hands. Afterwards, putting his paws solemnly on my shoulder, he licked my face and then went away into the farm.'

This, then, was the beginning of a deeply personal and emotional iden-tification with the country between Windermere and Derwentwater,

A view across Esthwaite, painted in 1911

since the Potters had now abandoned Scotland for the Lake District, renting one large property after another, usually near Keswick, but from time to time returning to the large white early-Victorian house on the lake which had now reverted to the Old English local name of Ees Wyke, meaning 'house on the shore'. It was this area, in and around the village of Sawrey, that Beatrix loved best. She had made friends with young John Cannon and his wife at Hill Top and had become a familiar figure to their children, as well as to many others in the village. She had always had an aptitude for catching a child's attention, sharing her listener's delight in a simple story, and it may well have been the response of the Sawrey children, as well as of Noël Moore and his brother and sisters, that brought her to the point of wondering whether the adventures of Peter Rabbit might be turned into a book. Noël, as we have seen, still had the original letter and magnanimously lent it. Peter Rabbit himself at nine years old was still alive, though a little infirm, and Canon Rawnsley, now vicar of Crosthwaite near Keswick, was at hand during the summer holidays to give advice. And so the

Beatrix on holiday

idea of a modest book for children gradually took shape. The story, as told to Noël, was extended, the black-and-white pictures were redrawn and a number of fresh ones added, including a coloured frontispiece of Mrs Rabbit administering camomile tea to her resistant son.

Canon Rawnsley, being a man of letters and an irrepressible versifier on any and every occasion, knew the names of publishers and was able to supply at least six addresses to which the manuscript of *Peter Rabbit* was sent in turn. The first of these was Frederick Warne & Co., already known as prolific publishers of children's books. Their rejection differed from that of the others only in that it was courteously expressed.

Canon Rawnsley

Nobody seemed even faintly interested, and Beatrix, carefully considering that she now had a sum in the Post Office savings bank, decided to publish the little book herself.

Her idea of what a small child's book should be was both modest and practical. It should be small in itself, little more than five inches by four, printed on stout paper with a simple narrative and a picture every time one turned a page. But for all its simplicity it should not be namby-pamby; words were as important as pictures and she had no use for baby-talk; even the sparrows who overheard Peter Rabbit's sobs when he was caught in the gooseberry net 'flew to him in great excitement and implored him to exert himself.' Unexpected crumbs of information, too, it amused her to hide here and there under the surface of the text. Peter's search for parsley in Mr McGregor's garden when feeling 'rather sick' was not greedy but sensible: if Beatrix had consulted *Culpeper's Herbal* (with which she was almost certainly familiar) she would have found that parsley, according to that medical worthy, is 'very comfortable to the stomach', and that camomile tea, of which Mrs Rabbit administers a tablespoonful at bedtime, 'eases . . . all the pains and torments of the belly.' (It is quite likely that Mrs Cannon, too, being a farmer's wife, knew all about camomile tea, which was a traditional country remedy. Flora Thompson, writing in *Lark Rise* of cottage life in Oxfordshire in the 'eighties, remembered that cottagers' wives drank it freely 'to ward off colds and soothe the nerves, and as a general tonic.')

A view overlooking Derwentwater, inscribed 'September 3, 1907'

Encouraged by Canon Rawnsley (who was still optimistically bom-
barding Warnes with letters and even proffering his own rhymed version of *Peter Rabbit* in forty-one pages of dreadful verse) she approached
a printer whose name had been given her by someone at the Natural
History Museum, and the great project was set in motion. By December
1901 the little book was ready, an unpretentious edition of 250 copies
in grey-green covers ornamented with an outline drawing of four little
rabbits, and she was enjoying the pleasure of selling it in fours and fives

to her friends and relations at one-and-twopence a copy. 'It caused a good deal of amusement amongst my relations and friends. I made about £12 or £14 by selling copies to obliging aunts.' The aunts *were* obliging, and she bore this cautiously in mind: still, now that *Peter Rabbit* was actually published and looking so much more presentable under the flattery of binding and print, it was perhaps worth while just showing him to Warnes again. They had, according to their letter, been 'pleased with the designs', and were the only firm which had shown a glimmer of interest. The book was now selling so well (Conan Doyle had bought a copy for his children and had expressed approval) that she was thinking of a second small edition, and in February 1902 a further two hundred were printed with an improved text. This second printing was in fact an interim measure, for Canon Rawnsley, abandoning verse, had still been busy in correspondence on the matter, acting, in fact, as a kind of unofficial literary agent, and Warnes now offered

Sheep in a meadow. Undated Lake District watercolour

A variant of the frontispiece to
The Tale of Peter Rabbit:
Mrs Rabbit giving a dose of
camomile to Peter

to publish what they called her 'quaint little book' themselves if she would do coloured illustrations instead of black-and-white. Incidentally, as they cautiously added in a postscript, 'We very much prefer your own letterpress to the verses by Canon Rawnsley.'

This may have caused a momentary embarrassment, but the Canon was busy and remote in Cumberland and Beatrix could undertake the correspondence herself. 'I do not know,' she wrote in one of her early letters to the firm, 'if it is necessary to consult Canon Rawnsley; I should think *not*.' – and from then on the thrilling enterprise was her own. Except, of course, that as the matter progressed there were questions of copyright and royalties and the price at which the little book could be sold, and there was a danger that Mr Potter might enter the scene. 'I have not spoken to Mr Potter,' she added somewhat nervously at the end of a letter, 'but I think, Sir, it would be well to explain the agreement clearly because he is a little formal, having been a barrister.' And the following spring, when she had spent a fortnight with Bertram at his Roxburgh farm, working hard to improve the *Peter Rabbit* drawings, there was a possibility that Papa might actually accompany her to the publisher's offices in Bedford Street to go over the clauses of the contract. 'If my father happens to insist on going with me to see the agreement, would you please not mind him very much, if he is very fidgety about things – I am afraid it is not a very respectful way of talking and I don't wish to refer to it again, but I think it is better to mention beforehand that he is sometimes a little difficult. I can of course do what I like about the book being 3s. I suppose it is a habit of old gentlemen, but sometimes rather trying.'

The letters from the publishers, at first meticulously formal and always signed 'Dear Madam, Yours faithfully, Frederick Warne & Co.,' now became more relaxed in tone and sometimes, beside the corporate signature, bore inconspicuous initials, NDW. These were the mark of Norman Warne, youngest and only unmarried son of the firm, who had been deputed to deal with the *Peter Rabbit* material. When eventually Beatrix visited Bedford Street to examine the proofs she found him gentle and shy, not at all alarming, and from this point their discussions of her drawings went on in an easy, critical and friendly spirit. 'My brother is sarcastic about the figures,' she wrote from Roxburgh, where she was struggling to improve her images of Mr and Mrs McGregor. (The human figure was for some reason always beyond her, as she was the first to acknowledge.) 'What you and he take for Mr McGregor's nose, was intended for his ear, not his nose at all . . . The people are very

The pose of Peter Rabbit in this illustration
has obvious similarities with the pose of the child in Anne Merritt's
popular painting, 'Love Locked Out'

This watercolour of Trafalgar Square, by H. M. Marshall,
dated 1890, gives an impression of the London scene in the 'nineties.
It belonged to Mrs Rupert Potter, who acquired it in 1896.

suitable here, if one were not afraid of them; especially the cook . . . I
never learnt to draw figures . . . and am very glad that you have sent
them back.' Norman Warne had rejected the inadequate figure of Mrs
McGregor in the private edition (opposite Mrs Rabbit's sinister warning – 'Your father had an accident there; he was put in a pie by Mrs
McGregor') and Beatrix was now stalking Bertram's cook as a model,
but without success. In the end she compromised, none too well, with
a self-caricature which appeared in the first Warne edition but was
subsequently abandoned. There were other difficulties too, even with
the rabbits. 'I wish that the drawings had been better . . . I am sorry to
have made such a muddle of them. Peter died at 9 years old, just before
I began the drawings, and now when they are finished I have got
another young rabbit, and the drawings look wrong.'

But at last, by the late summer of 1902, just as the Potters were setting off for their three months at Ees Wyke, the book was all but ready and the author received her final proofs at Sawrey. She was to earn no royalty on the first three thousand copies of the shilling edition, but after that a royalty of 1¼ d. a copy. Modest as this seemed, it was an intoxicating experience to realize that she had at last achieved something on her own, and as the sales steadily rose and pirated editions, to her astonishment, appeared in America, she began turning over other possibilities in her mind, remembering the tales and rhymes that she had loved as a child, and the spontaneous stories with which she had delighted other children. It was the direct, unpremeditated approach, she began to see, that was the secret of success. This was surely the only way to account for the unexpected, the altogether undreamed-of success of *Peter Rabbit*. 'It is much more satisfactory,' she wrote a few years later, remembering her impromptu picture-letters to the little Moores, 'to address a real live child. I often think that was the secret of the success of *Peter Rabbit*; it was written to a child – not made to order.'

The previous winter, at the time when she was anxiously waiting for her privately printed edition, Beatrix Potter had written, as a special Christmas present for Freda Moore, an account of the mouse story she had heard when staying with Caroline Hutton near Gloucester. She had been to Harescombe Grange several times since that first occasion of six years ago, and on each visit had made a point of sketching scenes and details which might be useful if she ever decided to build them into a story; even sitting down on a doorstep, her cousin remembered, to sketch the street for a snow-scene, in spite of the fact that it was the height of summer. Only one detail had she omitted to record, and that was the interior of the tailor's shop, where the old man had sat cross-legged on his long table, working against the clock on the mayor's waistcoat. This scene, however, presented itself as though by magic in London, when she found herself passing a tailor's shop in Chelsea and saw through the window another old man at work in the traditional posture. Walking quickly past, she pulled a button off her coat and went back to the shop, where the tailor carried out this small repair. While he sewed she carefully observed the shabby interior, tools of the trade and scraps and snippets littered about the table, which she sketched from memory as soon as she got home.

Now, in time for the Christmas of 1901 she had written out the tale, interspersed with nursery rhymes, in an exercise book with twelve watercolour pictures pasted in, and packed it up for Freda with a dedicatory letter. 'Because you are fond of fairy-tales and have been ill, I have made you a story all for yourself – a new one that nobody has read before.' At the end she added – conscious perhaps that there were too many words and too few pictures for a child – 'There ought to be more pictures towards the end, and they would have been the best ones; only Miss Potter was tired of it! Which was lazy of Miss Potter.'

Certainly there were too many nursery rhymes for the balance of the story, but Miss Potter had a passion for them, and chose her favourites from the Victorian collections that she had known all her life, Halliwell's *Nursery Rhymes of England* and Walter Crane's *The Baby's Opera* and *The Baby's Bouquet*; the excuse being that 'It is in the old story, that all the beasts can talk in the night between Christmas Eve and Christmas Day in the morning.' In Freda's handwritten version the beasts are perpetually singing; they overwhelm the story with their ditties and the enchanting legend of the poor old tailor, his cat Simpkin and the accomplished mice who do his finishing work for him, is obscured by repetitive nursery rhymes and jingles.

A year later, when the Warne edition of *Peter Rabbit* was about to be published, Beatrix Potter decided on a second private enterprise with *The Tailor of Gloucester*. She felt that to propose a second book to Warnes so soon might seem pretentious; besides, she had a shrewd idea that they would insist on reducing the number of nursery rhymes, of which she was personally so fond. So it seemed best to go ahead with the printers she had employed before, borrowing the copy-book back from Freda, redrawing ten of the twelve pictures and adding six more. Then, feeling nervous that he might hear of the project from another source, she wrote to Norman Warne. 'I will send you the little mouse-book as soon as it is printed . . . Except the children's rough copy I have not shown it to anyone as I was rather afraid people might laugh at the words. I thought it a very pretty story when I heard it in the country, but it has proved rather beyond my capacity for working out . . .'

An edition of five hundred copies was ready by the middle of December and Norman Warne duly received his, together with a hint that she was planning another story, this time about squirrels. His response was encouraging: they were prepared to consider *The Tailor* and possibly the squirrel book as well, although he was afraid there would have to be some excisions. 'I perceive that your criticisms are just', Beatrix Potter replied, 'because I was quite sure in advance that you would cut out the tailor and all my favourite rhymes! Which was one of the reasons why I printed it myself . . . I think,' she added at the end, looking forward without enthusiasm to the Potter family Christmas, 'my sympathies are still with the poor old tailor,' but she could well believe the squirrel book 'would be more likely to appeal to people who are accustomed to a more cheerful Christmas than I am.'

In spite of her forebodings – 'I am afraid it is going to fall rather flat here' – the privately printed edition of *The Tailor of Gloucester* sold encouragingly well. Still better, naturally, when Warnes had taken it over, with the nursery rhymes drastically reduced and (but this was a pity) her picture of the rollicking rats in the mayor's cellar, actually putting a bottle of wine to their whiskered lips, eliminated out of respect for the Sunday schools and temperance movement. ('For the life of me,' Beatrix Potter wrote many years later, 'I could not see why Mr Warne insisted on cutting it out.') One response, which both astonished and delighted her, was a long and favourable review in *The Tailor and Cutter*. Miss Potter had remembered to send a copy to the Chelsea tailor, and when she called in to see if he had liked it, he told her that he had lent his copy to a traveller from *The Tailor and Cutter* and 'they had put in a beautiful review!' The review indeed was enthusiastic, and must have sent up the sales of the book among responsive tailors. 'We think it is far the prettiest story connected with tailoring that we have ever read.' They were 'even not ashamed to confess that it brought the moisture to our eyes, as well as the smile to our face.'

Their praise was justified. The rhyme-choked version which had been written for Freda Moore had, under Norman Warne's tactful suggestion, been both pruned and enriched. A great deal of work had gone into the improvement of the pictures, and Beatrix had found, poring anxiously over the cases in the South Kensington Museum, that she had only to ask the clerk to have garments and embroideries taken out of their cases and spread out for her to copy in one of the offices. These amenities, and her own tame mice who obliged as working models, contributed enormously to the success of the finished work, which many people regard – as indeed she did herself – as her masterpiece, or at least her 'favourite among the little books'.

The illustration to The Tailor of Gloucester, *on the right, was based on the watercolour of a fireplace at Melford Hall (opposite) which had been drawn by Beatrix Potter some years earlier*

The watercolour of carousing rats which Beatrix Potter did for the original edition of The Tailor of Gloucester, *but which was omitted from Warnes' published edition*

(left) *The frontispiece to* The Tailor of Gloucester. *(right)* *Detail from* Hogarth's *'Noon' on which Beatrix Potter based the frontispiece to* The Tailor of Gloucester

Exquisite as it is, it is not everyone's favourite. The frontispiece, translated with disastrous sentimentality from Hogarth's 'Noon', is a prime example of the kind of thing that Beatrix Potter could not do. Her human figures are almost always a failure; but the moment she is among mice, and cats, and cottage interiors, and beautiful embroidery, she has no equal; and it is not surprising that many people, introduced in early childhood to this unforgettable jewel of a book, should think of Gloucester chiefly as a city that once had a tailor, and where the mice were caught short in their rescue operation because there was 'no more twist'.

The real tailor, by the way, he whose loyal assistants started the whole story, was one John Samuel Prichard, who lived until 1934, and on the kerbstone of whose grave in the churchyard of Charlton Kings bears the inscription 'The Tailor of Gloucester'.

The crags and valleys around Derwentwater, where the Potters now often spent the summer, are grander and more dramatic than the gentle farming country around Sawrey. 'I prefer a pastoral landscape backed by mountains . . .' Beatrix had once written in her journal. 'It really strikes me that some scenery is almost theatrical, or ultra-romantic.' Still, the vision of the lake from Lingholm, the house which they often occupied, was hauntingly beautiful, craggy mountains rising behind the lake and St Herbert's Island lying green and wooded in the great expanse of water. Beatrix had more than once made watercolour sketches of the scene, and now that her mind was busy with possible ideas for further books, all of which she could discuss with Norman Warne by letter, she suddenly saw St Herbert's as Owl Island, and the perfect setting for a squirrel story.

As early as 1897 she had relayed to Noël Moore a legend about squirrels ferrying themselves across water on rafts of bark (she seems to have come across this somewhere in a book about Canadian forests) and had also heard something at Keswick which appeared to support the story. 'There is a lady who lives on an island on the lake who told me some curious things about animals swimming. She had a cat which she did not want, so she gave it to someone in Keswick, but a week afterwards it came back into the house dripping wet! Also when her nuts are ripe, squirrels appear on the island, but she has not seen them coming. There is an American story that squirrels go down the rivers on little rafts, using their tails for sails, but I think the Keswick squirrels must swim.' The Keswick squirrels were, of course, the indigenous red variety, now found only in isolated areas, not the American grey squirrel which proliferates almost everywhere.

At Lingholm again in 1901 she had been so much amused by 'a most comical little squirrel' who had lost most of his tail and 'was so impertinent, he chattered and clattered and threw down acorns on to my head' – that, writing to Norah Moore, she had quickly sketched the scene in a corner of the letter. It was a very long letter, full of pictures and verses and a most convincing account of how the insufferable squirrel – 'I believe that his name was Nutkin and that he had a brother called Twinkleberry' – had deservedly lost his tail. Nine-year-old Norah, of course, had kept the letter and it was borrowed back, so that a busy exchange of letters was soon going on between Bolton Gardens and Bedford Street as *Squirrel Nutkin* was revised and groomed for publication.

The influence of Norman Warne, in encouraging Beatrix Potter's own creative style of expression, should not be minimized. It was his good critical sense, as well as the reactions of her child cousins, which weaned her away from depending too much on nursery rhymes and riddles. 'The words of the squirrel book will need cutting down, to judge by the children here,' she wrote from Melford Hall in Suffolk –

(*left*) *The frontispiece to*
The Tale of Squirrel Nutkin

(*right*) *The illustration to*
The Tale of Squirrel Nutkin
*showing the squirrels 'on little
rafts, using their tails for sails'*

week afterwards it came back into her
house dripping wet!

Also when her nuts are ripe, squirrels
appear on the island, but she has
not seen them coming. There is an
American story that squirrels go down
the rivers on
little rafts,
using their
tails

for sails, but
I think the Keswick squirrels must
swim. I must write to Eric next time
I hope you are quite well again. I remain
dear Noël yrs aff —

Beatrix Potter.

Part of a letter from Beatrix Potter to Noël Moore

The Warne family enjoying themselves. Norman is on the left; Millie next to him

still red-squirrel country, by the way – where she was staying with the Hyde-Parkers. 'I have got several good hints about the words.' And presently, again to Norman, 'I believe you were right about those rhymes; I will take them out.' The riddles with which the bad-mannered Nutkin exasperates Old Brown, the owl on whose permission to gather nuts the squirrels depend, are of course part of the amusement of the story, but in the early stages, as with the carols and ditties in *The Tailor of Gloucester*, there had been too many. As the text of the book, usually following Norman Warne's suggestions, was gradually pruned and shaped, so her own shrewd economical style triumphantly emerged. She would not in future depend on riddles and rhymes. Like Squirrel Nutkin, Miss Potter had learned her lesson.

In the same way, gaining confidence in herself as the drawings progressed, she escaped from her old desire to imitate Randolph Caldecott. In 1902, when she was finishing the Warne version of *Peter Rabbit* and thinking of following it up with a book of traditional rhymes, she wrote, 'I will try to bring one of the frames of Caldecott's to Bedford

Street in the autumn. I have been looking at them a good deal . . . It may sound odd to talk about mine and Caldecott's at the same time; but I think I could at least try to do better than *Peter Rabbit*.' What she had in mind was something 'in a style between Caldecott's and *The Baby's Opera*,' but fortunately, now that the Derwent squirrels had come on the scene, Caldecott's popular sentimental stereotype was abandoned and she was as deeply absorbed in squirrel-watching as any dedicated naturalist.

The tame squirrels kept by a friend had for some reason proved unsatisfactory and the gamekeeper at Melford Hall had failed to trap her a specimen, so she had been obliged to buy a couple from a dealer. 'I have got a very pretty little model,' she wrote early in 1903; 'I bought two but they weren't a pair, and fought so frightfully that I had to get rid of the handsomer and most savage one. The other squirrel is rather

Norman Warne with a nephew

Squirrel burying nuts; believed to be a wood near Derwentwater which served as the background to Squirrel Nutkin. *This is dated about 1903*

a nice little animal, but half of one ear has been bitten off, which spoils his appearance!'

The owl, too, gave trouble at first; those at the Zoo were somehow not quite right; it was Bertram's owl that dominated Old Brown's image – severe, inscrutable, sitting with a mouse's tail hanging out of his mouth. 'I am going to meet my brother at the Lakes,' she wrote in March, '. . . I think *he* could very likely improve that owl.' She was working hard on the book and, delighted with her publisher's suggestion, designing endpapers which could be used in subsequent editions.

The chief frustration at this time was the ritual moving about of the Potter family: the two weeks' exodus at Easter was 'a very vexatious interruption of work', and there were ominous signs, besides, that her parents were becoming restive about her correspondence with Warnes and occasional visits to Bedford Street.

By August 1903 *The Tale of Squirrel Nutkin* was in the shops, selling at a shilling, and proved an immediate success. 'I am *delighted* to hear such a good account of Nutkin,' Beatrix wrote. 'I never thought when I was drawing it that it would be such a success – though I think you always had a good opinion of it.' The good opinion of children soon began to arrive by post, to her great pleasure. 'I have had such comical letters from the children about "scell nuckin",' she wrote to Norman Warne, '. . . it seems an impossible word to spell; but they say they have "red" it right through, and that it is "lovely" – which is satisfactory. I shall always have a preference for cheap books myself – even if they did not pay; all my little friends happen to be shilling people. I do dislike,' she added, 'the modern fashion of giving children heaps of expensive things which they don't look at twice.'

She had several ideas for other books which she was eager to discuss, but suddenly, it seems, the Potter parents put their foot down and the exodus to the north was prepared for in an atmosphere of silent disapproval. 'I have to apologise for not having answered your letter,' Beatrix wrote in haste before leaving, 'and I regret that I cannot call again at the office before leaving town. If I had not supposed that the matter would be dealt with through the post, I should not have mentioned the subject of another book at present. I have had such painful unpleasantness at home . . . about the work that I should like a rest from scolding while I am away. I should be obliged if you would kindly say no more about a new book at present.'

6

THE DOLL'S HOUSE

In less than a fortnight, however, letters were posting backwards and forwards as eagerly as before, marvellously brightening the endless summer holiday which, as Beatrix allowed herself to confess, 'is always a weary business'. Even the long summer of 1903, spent with her parents at a large country house overlooking Derwentwater, was now alive with private interest and excitement, for the little books so far had done remarkably well (*Squirrel Nutkin* was selling in tens of thousands and was about to go into a third printing) and everything presented itself as a possible scene or idea for another story. 'I am rather surprised to hear about "Nutkin" ', she wrote to Norman Warne after receiving an unexpectedly fat cheque; 'it seems a great deal of money for such little books. I cannot help thinking it is a good deal owing to your spreading them about so well.' And at the end of the letter, following her formal 'kind regards' and signature, she could not resist adding, 'It is pleasant to feel I could earn my own living.'

There were many signs, quite apart from the sales, that her little books were marvellously popular with children, and that Peter Rabbit and Nutkin in particular had become nursery heroes. Stuffed Peter Rabbits made of velvet and fur had appeared at Harrods; Mr Potter had himself seen, and bought, a squirrel labelled 'Nutkin' in the Burlington Arcade, and a tiresome lady, who seems never to have heard of the tricky question of copyright, was proposing to design a nursery wallpaper with a frieze of Beatrix Potter animals. Astonished and delighted by these signs of success (though she was understandably irritated by the wallpaper lady) Beatrix prudently put the money in the bank and began to think seriously of buying herself 'an expensive present'. What this was, she at first kept secret from everyone except Norman Warne and the bank manager. It was more than a year before she actually achieved it – a small field in Sawrey, of so modest an acreage that in a letter to Warnes she described herself as going round it with a tape-measure. 'I shall pay part of the price on Dec. 1st and there will remain to pay in the future a sum of £300 at 4%, which need not

cause me any anxiety as the books are doing so well.' It gave her in-
expressible pleasure to own even so small a fragment of the village she
had come to love, and the feeling was deepened by the satisfaction of
having bought it with her own money. Her parents, it seems, were at
first not informed of the purchase, but when sooner or later they had
to be told it would be explained to them not – heaven forbid! – as a
first tentative experiment in independence, but as a prudent investment.

Everything, now, was full of interest. The obsessive sketching and
drawing which had filled so many idle days now had a purpose; back-
grounds, trees, gardens, banks and rabbit holes might well provide the
scenery for another drama. The children of Sawrey in particular had
become so devoted to *Peter Rabbit* that she began to wonder whether
she had been a little too ambitious with *Nutkin* and *The Tailor*; the
latter, after all, as she remembered, had been 'most in request amongst
old ladies.' A sequel to *Peter Rabbit* was what her little village friends
demanded. 'I sometimes feel afraid,' she wrote to Norman, 'that the
Tailor and Nutkin are rather too ingenious and complicated compared
with Peter Rabbit; don't you think the next one ought to be more
simple?' She was thinking of Peter's predecessor, her own impudent
and vigorous Benjamin Bunny, who she felt quite sure would make a
suitable hero.

Norman Warne agreed, and the summer of 1903, spent at Fawe Park
near Keswick, was devoted to sketching the garden and surrounding
woods, the pear tree on the wall of the kitchen garden, the cucumber
frames and potting-shed where Mr McGregor (not the resident gardener
but a more or less imaginary person) would be constantly on the watch
for marauding rabbits. 'I think I have done every imaginable rabbit
background,' she wrote to Norman Warne, 'and miscellaneous sketches
as well – about seventy! I hope you will like them, though rather
scribbled.' Her new rabbit model, a female, was full of spirit. 'I had
a funny instance of rabbit ferocity last night. I had been playing with
the ferret, and then with the rabbit without washing my hands. She,
the rabbit, is generally a most affectionate little animal but she simply
flew at me, biting my wrist all over before I could fasten the hutch.
Our friendship is at present restored with scented soap.'

The story was to be a true sequel to *Peter Rabbit*, involving the rescue
of Peter's lost clothing from Mr McGregor's garden and the theft of
some onions, the raid being organized by Peter's more courageous

cousin, Benjamin Bunny. Mr and Mrs McGregor having gone off for the day in a gig, the rabbits assume they have the place to themselves, until by an evil chance they encounter a cat, who sits for five hours on the basket under which they are hidden. Anxiety at home in the warren is intense, but all is well at last when old Mr Bunny comes to the rescue, scares off the cat (as an experienced buck rabbit is quite capable of doing), whips the two truants and drives them back in disgrace to the

(opposite) Study of a water-tub drawn at Fawe Park, Keswick in 1903, adapted for the illustration to Benjamin Bunny *(above)*

rabbit hole. Peter's mother forgives him, hanging up the onions from her kitchen beams together with her bunches of herbs and rabbit-tobacco (lavender), and the story thus happily ended is dedicated by the author 'To the children of Sawrey, from old Mr Bunny'.

Every detail, both of narrative and pictures, was discussed as the tale progressed, and it is clear from Beatrix Potter's letters at this time that it meant much to her to have someone taking an amused yet serious

8 Bedford Square, home of the Warne family

Mrs Frederick Warne, wearing (for the camera)
an uncharacteristically severe expression

interest in her work; someone, moreover, who had become a personal
friend as well as her publisher. It was the friendship part of it that had
caused the trouble with her parents, since her businesslike visits to
Bedford Street (almost always accompanied by a female acquaintance
from the museum who acted as chaperone) had led to some happily
informal visits to No. 8 Bedford Square, which was still the principal
home of the Warne family. The publishing house had always been a
family business. Frederick Warne, the founder, had retired in 1894,
leaving the firm in the hands of his three sons, Harold, Fruing and
Norman. Harold and Fruing were married and the fathers of families,
living respectively at Surbiton and Primrose Hill and travelling daily to
the office in Bedford Street by train. Norman, the youngest son and
still unmarried, lived with his mother and sister in the large and cheerful
house in Bedford Square which was still the centre of continuous family
activities. There were nearly always children in the house, either staying or visiting, and 'Uncle Norman' was a favourite with them all.
Mrs Frederick, whom Beatrix discovered with relief to be a merry-
tempered old lady in a white lace cap, welcomed her warmly into

(*above*) *Study of onions, inscribed 'August 30, '03'; clearly a preparation for the various onion pictures in* Benjamin Bunny (*right*). '*Then he suggested that they should fill the pocket-handkerchief with onions, as a little present for his Aunt.*'

the family circle, even seeming to approve of her growing friendship with Norman, since it was one of her basic beliefs that everyone should be married.

Norman himself, like Beatrix Potter, was shy, self-contained and unobtrusive. He, too, was at his best with children and spent much of his leisure in devising treats and pastimes for his nephews and nieces. He collected butterflies, organized magic-lantern shows for tea parties, dressed up in white beard and red flannel on Christmas Eve, and in the large untidy basement which he used as a workshop designed and per-fected all sorts of ingenious constructions – glass-fronted mouse-cages with ladders and bedrooms, and some astonishingly elaborate doll's houses. His latest masterpiece in this genre was a magnificent red-brick suburban villa about four feet high which he had made for his niece Winifred, Fruing's small daughter. There were lace curtains in all the windows, rooms on three separate floors and a tower with a round window. Beatrix had seen this extravagant toy during the later stages of construction in the basement workshop, but by the time it had occurred to her that it would be the perfect setting for a story about a pair of house-mice the doll's house had already been moved to the nursery at Surbiton.

This ought not to have been a problem, since Warnes were enthusi-astic about her idea and Norman was eager to take her to his brother's home, where she could make all the drawings she needed. But here, it seems, Mrs Potter created an unpleasant atmosphere, and the expedition had to be abandoned: Beatrix would have to make do with photo-graphs. The mice themselves were already part of her usual third-floor company, and could be studied at home. They had been caught in a cage-trap in the kitchen at Harescombe Grange during one of her visits to the Huttons and she had rescued them from the cook and brought them to London. The box she proposed to keep them in had proved 'rickety', and she had asked Norman Warne, whose small nephews and nieces had nicknamed him 'Johnny Crow' after one of their favourite picture-book characters (a resourceful bird who was always helpful to everybody), to make her a more practical model. 'I wish "Johnny Crow" would make my mouse "a little house"; do you think he would if I made a paper plan? I want one with glass at the side before I draw Hunca Munca again.' (She had named her new acquisitions Tom Thumb and Hunca Munca after the hero and heroine of Fielding's eighteenth-century burlesque, *Tom Thumb the Great*.) The mouse-cage had obligingly been made – 'I have had so very much pleasure with that box, I am never tired of watching them run up and down' – and in the intervals of finishing *Benjamin Bunny* she was making sketches of the inmates.

And now, just when she was ready to study the doll's house in all its detail, there was this sudden difficulty about going to Surbiton. 'I was very much perplexed about the doll's house,' Beatrix wrote to Norman Warne, 'and I should be so *very* sorry if Mrs Warne or you thought me uncivil. I did not think I could manage to go to Surbiton without staying lunch; I hardly ever go out, and my mother is so exacting I had not enough spirit to say anything about it. I have felt vexed with myself since, but did not know what to do. It does wear a person out . . . As far as the book is concerned I think I can do it from the photograph and my box; but it is very hard to have seemed uncivil.'

Mrs Fruing Warne at once suggested that it would be delightful if Mrs Potter would accompany Norman and Beatrix to Surbiton and have lunch with the family, but this, as Beatrix knew only too well, was out of the question. 'I don't think that my mother would be very likely to go to Surbiton,' she wrote mournfully to Norman, 'you did not understand what I meant by "exacting". People who only see her

The doll's house made by Norman Warne which
was the model for the one in The Tale of Two Bad Mice

Mrs Potter and a friend

casually do not know how disagreeable she can be when she takes dislikes. I should have been glad enough to go. I did not know what to do . . .' Clearly Mrs Potter had taken a dislike to the whole Warne family, since publishers in her view were simply tradesmen, and therefore much below what Beatrix herself called 'people of our station'. (Although, as she wrote privately to Caroline Hutton, 'Publishing books is as clean a trade as spinning cotton.') It had not escaped Mrs Potter's notice that Beatrix and Norman Warne were corresponding almost daily; that her professional visits to the publishing house gave her pleasure, and that she came home from afternoons in Bedford Square in unusually good spirits. This obviously, to Mrs Potter's way

Beatrix's version of the doll's house,
as it appeared in Two Bad Mice, *with the dolls bought*
by Norman Warne in Seven Dials

of thinking, simply would not do. If Beatrix were ever allowed to
marry it must be into a wealthy family like the Huttons or the Gaddums
or the Hyde-Parkers, long established in impressive country houses and
with humble beginnings in cotton mills or elsewhere conveniently forgotten. She therefore set herself resolutely against any idea of a closer
friendship between Beatrix and Norman, and the atmosphere of Bolton
Gardens deteriorated accordingly. Mr Potter undoubtedly supported
his wife in this, but it is perhaps worth recording that in disagreeable
domestic campaigns of this sort it was Mrs rather than Mr Potter who
took the lead. Marjorie Moore, to whom as a child Beatrix Potter on
more than one occasion gave a summer holiday in cottage lodgings
in Sawrey while the family was at Ees Wyke, still remembers that in
spite of his fierce expression Mr Potter could, and often did, unbend,

especially in the company of children, so that her recollection of him on those happy occasions was of 'a dear old man' – whereas Mrs Potter remained always disapproving, implacable, remote.

All this Beatrix, as a respectful and dutiful daughter, accepted as unfortunate but inevitable. The time had not yet come when she would assert herself, and for the present she had the consolation of work. 'I will manage to make a nice book somehow,' she told Norman. 'Hunca Munca is very ready to play the game; I stopped her in the act of carrying a doll as large as herself up to the nest. She cannot resist anything with lace or ribbon; she despises the dishes.'

The dishes were a sumptuous selection of doll's-house food, chosen by Norman at Hamleys and dispatched by post. He had also bought her a pair of dolls – 'just exactly what I wanted' – in the market at Seven Dials. 'The things will all do beautifully,' she wrote to him as soon as the parcels arrived; 'the ham's appearance is enough to cause indigestion. I am getting almost more treasures than I can squeeze into one small book.' His photographs of the interior of the doll's house, too, gave her more attractive details for the story. 'They are very good; and I have got an idea from the staircase and top floor. The inside view is amusing – the kind of house where one cannot sit down without upsetting something, I know the sort!'

Indeed she did, and in this enchanting little tale, which was very much a collaboration between Norman and herself, one sees some of the happiest and most perceptive aspects of her work. Mice are, after all, enchanting, highly skilled and intelligent animals, as most children know, and the theme of an ingenious pair invading a doll's house and becoming enraged by the discovery that the food is made of plaster and that the red crinkly-paper fire in the grate won't burn, is one of Beatrix Potter's happiest conceptions. The mice themselves are drawn in loving detail – quick, clever, destructive, acquisitive – and it seems utterly natural that in the end, having smashed the plates and torn the feathers out of the dolls' bolster, Hunca Munca (who 'had a frugal mind') should suddenly remember 'that she herself was in want of a feather bed'. So we see the bird-cage and the toy bookcase and the coal-scuttle and the cradle, together with a number of other useful objects and a selection of dolls' clothes, being carried off to the mouse-hole, and the expressionless shock suffered by the dolls when they return from their drive in the pram and find their house has been burgled.

But Beatrix Potter, quite rightly, did not end the story there. Mice have their own domestic virtues, which she interpreted by showing Hunca Munca with her litter of baby mice tucked up in the cradle, her kitchen and wardrobe well equipped and her conscience appeased by coming early every morning, before anybody is awake, 'with her dust-pan and her broom to sweep the Dollies' house.' This is one of her most light-hearted books, and Norman Warne's contribution to its delightful atmosphere is everywhere apparent. The mice, too, had provided their own kind of inspiration, for they had been a pleasure and amusement to draw, and now that *Benjamin Bunny* was finished she was 'glad to get done with rabbits.' Why should they not, she asked Norman Warne, consider another mouse book? She would collect or make up some rhymes to match the pictures, and Hunca Munca would willingly oblige as model for 'Appley-Dapply, a little brown mouse.' (This was not to appear in book form for another thirteen years, but she was already making new sketches of mice and sending them to Norman.) The fascination which her mice held for her as subjects both of study and fantasy was something which remained with her to the end of her life. Hunca Munca came to a sad end a year after her immortalization in *The Tale of Two Bad Mice*, but her character, and that of her husband Tom Thumb, was still being celebrated a number of years later in the miniature letters to children (tiny facsimiles of grown-up notes, sealed and stamped and sent in a stitched mailbag) with which she was amusing herself and them as late as 1912. Here, with the antecedent instructions from the Doll's House, is Hunca Munca's only surviving holograph:

Mrs Tom Thumb, Mouse Hole.

Miss Lucinda Doll will be obliged if Hunca Munca will come half an hour earlier than usual on Tuesday morning, as Tom Kitten is expected to sweep the kitchen chimney at 6 o'clock. Lucinda wishes Hunca Munca to come not later than 5.45 a.m.

Miss Lucinda Doll, Doll's House.

Honoured Madam,
I have received your note for which I thank you kindly, informing me that T. Kitten will arrive to sweep the chimney at 6. I will come punctually at 7. Thanking you for past favours I am, honoured Madam, your obedient humble Servant,

Hunca Munca.

*Sketch of mice drawn in 1905 by Beatrix Potter
for a collection of nursery rhymes which was eventually published with the
title* Appley Dapply's Nursery Rhymes, *1917*

The final illustration to The Tale of Two Bad Mice: *Hunca Munca arriving
'with her dustpan and her broom to sweep the Dollies' house'.*

In this busy spring of 1904, with *Benjamin Bunny* and *The Two Bad
Mice* approaching publication, so many ideas for future stories presented
themselves that she could hardly bear to stop. Her publisher's suggestion
that she might illustrate a children's book by another writer was not
for a moment considered. 'I have a strong feeling that every outside
book which I did, would prevent me from finishing one of my own.
I enjoy inventing stories – any number – but I draw so slowly and
laboriously that there are sure to be favourites of my own left undone
at the end of my working life-time, whether short or long.' A diversion
of this kind was unthinkable; the family summer exodus was approaching and she was anxious to have her next subject – could it be Mrs
Tiggy-winkle? – settled before she left London. 'I think "Mrs Tiggy"
would be all right,' she wrote to Norman Warne. 'It is a *girls'* book; so
is the Hunca Munca; but there must be a large audience of little girls.'

Mrs Tiggy approved of, she went off in a happier frame of mind to the Lakes, cheered by the thought that her earnings might one day enable her to do something substantial for the little Moores. 'I am going to send one of the little girls to college some day,' she told Norman Warne, 'either Norah of the squirrel book or Freda; but there is time enough yet.' Arrived with her parents in the Lakes, however, she delayed starting on the new work, as though she missed the stimulus of Norman's criticism. 'I have not begun on the hedgehog book yet, I am ashamed to say,' she wrote at the end of two months, preparing to return, 'but I think it is not a bad thing to take a holiday. I have been working very industriously drawing fossils . . . upon the theory that a change of work is the best sort of rest! But I shall be quite keen to get back to work on the books again. If we get back on Saturday I might perhaps call on Tuesday morning?'

Benjamin Bunny and *The Two Bad Mice* were selling as successfully as their predecessors, the former having even had reviews in *The Times* and *The Scotsman*. (*The Times* had loftily decided that 'Miss Potter's fancy is not what it was. The story is inconclusive. Next year we think she must call in a literary assistant' – to which Miss Potter's sensible reaction was, 'I think it is a mistake to attend to them at all.') She had ordered a quantity to be sent to 'the little people at Sawrey. I am much vexed,' she added, 'to hear that more than half of them are down with

Another early mouse drawing used as the basic design for the picture of Hunca Munca and her family in The Tale of Two Bad Mice

scarlet fever and the school shut. I hope it is not the bad sort. I must stipulate that there are to be no letters of thanks!'

The winter was spent in her top-floor refuge in Bolton Gardens, working out scenes for the story which she had originally made up in 1902 for her cousin Stephanie. Her own beloved Mrs Tiggy-winkle had in the process become imaginatively identified with the old washer-woman employed at Dalguise House during those Scottish holidays which had meant so much to her as a child. In 1892, when she was twenty-six and staying with her parents in the same area, she had made a point of visiting Kitty MacDonald and recording the occasion in her journal. 'Went out with the pony, first to see Kitty MacDonald, our old washerwoman . . . Kitty is eighty-three, but waken, and delightfully merry . . . She is a comical, round little old woman, as brown as a berry and wears a multitude of petticoats and a white mutch. Her memory goes back for seventy years and I really believe she is prepared to enumerate the articles of her first wash in '71' – which was when the Potters had first gone there.

Kitty's starching and ironing, her pride in her work and her clean old-fashioned kitchen where the hot iron rested on an upturned horse-shoe, had seemed the perfect setting for Mrs Tiggy, and since in the last year or two Miss Potter had made friends with a little girl called Lucie Carr, daughter of the vicar of Newlands, near Keswick, she now decided to bring her into the story.

'Mrs Tiggy as a model is comical,' she wrote to Norman Warne. 'So long as she can go to sleep on my knee she is delighted, but if she is propped up on end for half an hour, she first begins to yawn pathetic-ally, and then she *does* bite! Nevertheless she is a dear person; just like a very fat, rather stupid little dog.' The difficulty of keeping Mrs Tiggy awake in an upright position was solved by making a dummy, which had the added advantage that it could be dressed up in petticoats and apron, which the real Mrs Tiggy had always refused to tolerate. 'The hedgehog drawings are turning out very comical. I have dressed up a cotton-wool dummy figure for convenience of drawing the clothes. It is such a little figure of fun; it terrifies my rabbit; but Hunca Munca's always at pulling out the stuffing. I think it should make a good book,' she added, 'when I have learnt to draw the child.'

This human figure, as always, was a difficulty, and the drawings of Lucie were revised again and again for Norman's approval. 'I am not good – or trained –,' she confessed, 'in drawing human figures. They are a terrible bother to me when I have perforce to bring them into the pictures for my own little stories.' Try as she might, the figure of Lucie is the one weak point in an otherwise perfect book, in which Mrs Tiggy is a masterpiece of observation and the interiors reflect everything that Beatrix Potter loved about those clean, warm, stone-floored farmhouse kitchens of the Lakes. 'It was a very nice clean kitchen,' she had written in the original exercise-book version, 'with a grey-flagged floor and whitewashed walls and a wide fireplace and shining copper pans – just like any other Lakes kitchen, only the ceiling was *very* low and the pans were as little as you have in a doll's house.'

The original story was drastically pruned and shortened – no doubt following the suggestions of Norman Warne, for the exercise-book version is tediously long and loaded with rhymes and verses. The margins of the surviving manuscript are heavily marked in Beatrix Potter's hand: 'Shorten this . . . Leave out some . . . Shorten this page . . . Shorten . . .'

By the early summer of 1905 *The Tale of Mrs Tiggy-Winkle* was all but finished and she was beginning to dread the gap that would be left if no new theme had been approved before she and Norman went off on their separate holidays. 'I wish another book could be planned out before the summer, if we are going on with them,' she wrote at the beginning of June. 'I always feel very much lost when they are finished.' And a few weeks later – 'I enclose the remainder of Tiggy, regretfully . . . I do so *hate* finishing books, I would like to go on with them for years . . .' Her state of mind was not altogether happy; the atmosphere at home had not improved, but of course nothing could be said. And a few days before leaving for the family holiday in Wales she had been rash enough to let Hunca Munca perform her acrobatics on a chandelier, and now miserably blamed herself for the mouse's death. 'Poor Hunca Munca,' she wrote wretchedly to Norman, 'I cannot forgive myself for letting her tumble. I do so miss her. She fell off the chandelier; she managed to stagger up the staircase into your little house, but she died in my hand about ten minutes after. I think if I had broken my own neck it would have saved a deal of trouble.'

The first part of the Potter family holiday was spent at the village of Llanbedr in Merioneth, and here at last the communication came that

A watercolour sketch for Mrs Tiggy-winkle's kitchen, probably drawn in 1904 when Beatrix Potter made several background sketches for Mrs Tiggy-Winkle

(*above*) *Mrs Tiggy-winkle and Lucie, as they appeared in* The Tale,
with (*below*) *Beatrix Potter's preliminary rough sketch of the scene*

she had been longing for. Norman Warne, too shy perhaps to have spoken in her presence, made his formal proposal of marriage by letter, and was accepted.

They were both approaching forty, and one would have thought that this was the beginning of a new, happy and creative life. The doll's house had been the scene of their first complete collaboration; Beatrix Potter's work had matured and blossomed during those happy months of 1904 until now, with the new little book in sight, Mrs Tiggy-winkle was about to make her bow and to become a legendary figure. Everything, on the surface, promised well, but from this moment a painful struggle began which was to lead to a tragic and unforeseen conclusion.

Mr and Mrs Potter, as Beatrix wearily knew already, were totally opposed to the match. Respectful and dutiful towards her parents as she had always been, there was no question of screaming rows or confrontations. ('I always thought I was born to be a discredit to my parents,' she had once ruefully written in her journal, and now, it seemed, they tended to agree.) Her mind nevertheless was made up and the struggle carried on in unhappy silence. No announcement was made and almost nobody told, but Beatrix now firmly considered herself betrothed and wore her engagement ring. In the only surviving photograph of Norman Warne taken at this time he, too, is wearing a ring on the third finger of his left hand, so it is reasonable to suppose that they had exchanged tokens.

Happiness during these difficult weeks was to be found only in Bedford Square, where Mrs Warne and her daughter Millie and all the rest of the family welcomed Beatrix with sympathetic affection. In Surbiton, too, where the now famous doll's house was established in its glory, the children were told that henceforth they must call Miss Potter 'Auntie Bee'. In September Mrs Tiggy would burst upon the world as a nursery heroine and everything – away from the scowling gloom of Bolton Gardens – promised well.

These moments of happiness were brief. Norman Warne had never been strong, and now suddenly and mysteriously became ill. At first he refused to see a doctor, and when finally one was summoned it was discovered that he was in an advanced stage of leukaemia and beyond help. He died at the end of August, after an engagement lasting less than a month.

How Beatrix Potter struggled through what remained of the

summer is difficult to imagine. Almost no one had been told of her engagement; nothing, naturally, was said at home, where her best defence was to bury herself in her work, carrying on with *The Pie and the Patty-pan*, which had been roughly sketched out and planned with Norman while she was still absorbed in *Mrs Tiggy-Winkle*. Only to Millie Warne, to whom she had become very close, signing herself in letters 'your affectionate sister', was she able to indicate a little of what his loss had meant. 'I am sending you,' she wrote after Norman's funeral, 'a copy of the sketch I did the last evening in the barley-field at Llanbedr.' (It was here that Norman's written proposal had reached her.) 'I try to think of the golden sheaves, and harvest; he did not live long, but he fulfilled a useful happy life. I must try to make a fresh beginning next

Millie Warne

year.' And at the end of September, spending a few days with an aunt in Bath, she wrote again: 'I find the names of the streets rather melancholy here. Do you remember Miss Austen's *Persuasion*, with all the scenes and streets in Bath? It was always my favourite, and I read the end part of it again last July. On the 26th, the day after I got Norman's letter, I thought my story had come right, with patience and waiting, like Anne Elliot's did.'

No doubt there was consolation of a sort to be found in *Mrs Tiggy-Winkle*'s success, which Norman had not lived to see. Thirty thousand copies had been sold in the first few weeks and the heroine's name had already passed into the language as a symbolic expression of scrupulous domesticity. But even here there was an element of sadness. The real Mrs Tiggy-winkle was growing old; it was obvious that she was unlikely to live much longer. 'I am sorry to say that I am upset about poor Tiggy,' Beatrix wrote to Millie Warne. 'She hasn't seemed well the last fortnight and has begun to be sick, and she is so thin . . . I am afraid that the long course of unnatural diet and indoor life is beginning to tell on her. It is a wonder she has lasted so long. One gets very fond of a little animal. I hope she will either get well or go quickly.' But Tiggy did not get well, and a fortnight later – 'Poor little Tiggy . . . has got so dirty and miserable that I think it is better not to have her any longer . . . She has always been such a scrupulously clean little animal.' So Mrs Tiggy was gently put to sleep with chloroform and buried with grief under what is now the playground of the Bousfield Primary School, but was then the garden behind No. 2 Bolton Gardens.

*An unfinished sketch of Mrs Tiggy-winkle,
probably drawn in 1904*

7
SawREY AND ITS
AɲIMAL CHARACTERS

There is no doubt that the village of Sawrey, with the sudden possibility of being able to buy Hill Top Farm, did more than anything to
support Beatrix Potter through the melancholy autumn months of
1905. The painful struggle with her parents was over: Norman was
dead. The long strain and final shock had brought her very low, and
for some weeks she was miserably ill. But the urge to complete the
work they had begun together – a cat-and-dog story, *The Pie and the
Patty-pan*, had been planned – and the chance of making a future home
for herself in Sawrey gave her the needed stimulus for recovery.

It seemed almost like a manifestation of providence. Earlier in the
summer she had asked one of the servants at Ees Wyke to let her know
if they ever heard of a small farm in the neighbourhood coming on the
market, and now, like the granting of a wish in a fairy tale, came the
news that Hill Top itself would shortly be for sale. She acted quickly.
The price presumably was modest; the acreage was small and the house
little more than a cottage; the Cannons were tenant farmers and could
be given notice. The earnings from her books were bringing in suffi-
cient income to guarantee the price, supported by a little legacy from
her Aunt Burton, and the transaction was completed without loss of
time by a firm of Ambleside solicitors.

The idea that one day Hill Top would be her personal home was
certainly the private motive behind the purchase. Encouraged by Bertram, invisible as usual in his Roxburgh fastness but firm in support
when she appealed to him, Beatrix represented the acquisition as a
sound investment, and her parents made no objection. There was no
question, of course, of her being allowed to live there. Unmarried
daughters had none of the freedoms of their bachelor brothers, and Mrs
Potter had always made it clear that since housemaids occasionally left
or otherwise 'made difficulties', Beatrix in Bolton Gardens was indis-
pensable. But she could certainly employ a farm servant or 'hind' as it
was locally called, to do the work and manage the affairs of the farm,
herself inspecting the accounts on occasional visits.

At first it seemed the Cannons would be given notice, but this was distressing and, as it proved, unnecessary. As Beatrix Potter watched John Cannon valuing his own stock and implements, taking infinite pains not to charge her a penny more than the fair price, she realized that he and his family were a part of Hill Top, and suggested that they stay. The offer was gratefully accepted, so that the little farm now became, at least in spirit, a co-operative venture, with Miss Potter gradually improving the house and garden as cheques from Warnes came in, and John Cannon acting as her agent at cattle sales, buying sheep and pigs. If the Potter family were at Ees Wyke it was easy enough to supervise the improvements and alterations – a piped water supply, an extension built on to the house for the Cannons, so that Miss Potter could refurbish the place to her own liking – and if they were further away, say at Lingholm near Keswick, it was possible to make the journey to Sawrey by coach and to stay in lodgings in the village. On these occasions she boarded with the blacksmith and his wife, Mr and Mrs Satterthwaite, in the house called Belle Green in Smithy Lane, near the post office and village shop, the Tower Bank Arms and everything else of interest in the village. From here she could comfortably finish her sketches, not only of the interior of Hill Top, but also of the village street, the little front gardens crowded with marigolds, poppies, snapdragons and lilies, and indeed everything that she had chosen to illustrate the story which she and Norman had agreed to call *The Pie and the Patty-pan*, and which was her first whole-hearted celebration of the village of Sawrey. 'If the book prints well,' she had written to Norman in June, 'it will be my next favourite to the "Tailor".'

The original story had been conceived and written two years before, but had been set aside in favour of *Two Bad Mice*, since they had both decided that the narrative was rather thin, as indeed it was – a brief account of a cat-and-dog tea-party, in the course of which it appears that the little dog, rather than a suspected fox, had stolen three brown eggs. The whole thing had since been reshaped in the early part of the year and a larger format decided on, to do justice to the exuberant detail of the pictures. In these the village triumphantly comes to life, and the story itself concerns notable Sawrey characters. The 'pussy-cat called Ribby, who invited a little dog called Duchess to tea' was undoubtedly a Sawrey cat, like her cousin Mrs Tabitha Twitchit, who lived at Hill Top, where, as on most farms, several cats were necessary. Duchess, the bitch of a black Pomeranian pair belonging to the wife of the gardener at Ees Wyke, lived in one of the three Lakefield cottages near the big house, and was well known for her intelligence and pretty manners. In 1902 Beatrix Potter had made some drawings of the interior of the gardener's cottage, including the stone-floored larder with its shelves full of baskets, bottles, pickle-jars and crockery, and more than once had admired Duchess sitting up to beg with a lump of sugar on her nose while the gardener's wife counted nine before she was allowed to crunch it. In the story Beatrix Potter redistributed the houses, making Lakefield Cottage Ribby's home and giving Duchess the cottage called Buckle Yeat, which had a particularly attractive front garden and in those days served as the village post office.

The Pie and the Patty-pan was awaited with great eagerness in Sawrey, and when the published book, dedicated to two of the youngest Moore children, arrived in October 1905, splendid in its new large size though still priced at only a shilling, the inhabitants were able to identify every stone and corner. Today, anyone who cares to know what Hill Top looked like before Miss Potter bought and extended it has only to look at the frontispiece, in which Ribby in shawl and apron is carrying her butter and milk from the farm across the field where John Cannon's herd of cows is peacefully grazing. The whitewashed walls and stone-grey tiles, the modest porch roofed with great slabs of slate, the lean-to woodshed and wood-pile are seen against a delicate sky and the distant cloud-capped outline of Coniston Old Man. Apart from the unobtrusive wing built for the Cannons and the startling colours of modern garden imports such as rhododendrons, it is little different today. (There were a few pink rhododendrons in Hill Top garden even in 1906, as one can see from the illustrations to Tom Kitten.)

The interiors of the two cottages, both in colour and black-and-white, are preserved in enchanting detail; there is not a feature of cottage kitchen or parlour in those days that Beatrix Potter did not observe and love. She knew exactly what plants would stand in a row on those deep window-sills – geraniums, maidenhairs, flowering cactus, trailing campanula, 'Mind your own business', 'Busy Lizzie'. Every sofa under such a window is upholstered in horsehair, the shiny hardness softened with knitted shawls and down-filled cushions. (The picture of Duchess standing on Ribby's sofa and searching fruitlessly in the cupboard for the 'pie made of mouse' is so reminiscent of the Briton Riviere painting of

The frontispiece to The Pie and the Patty-pan *is
an accurate, and still largely unaltered,
view of Hill Top farm.*

(above) Ribby in the larder. An unfinished sketch. (below) Ribby going to the cupboard.
An unfinished sketch not used in the book

(*above*) *An unfinished sketch not used in the book.* (*below*) *Ribby welcoming Duchess. Another unfinished sketch not used in the book*

"A little more bacon, my dear Duchess?" said Ribby.
"Thank you, my dear Ribby; I was only feeling for the patty-pan."

her own little cousin Kate Potter that one cannot believe that in this cottage version Beatrix is not enjoying a private joke.)

Ribby's fireside, as she awaits her guest in her best lilac silk with muslin apron and tippet, is an epitome of all such comfortable cottage hearths – except that, being in a cat's house, there is more than the usual number of mousetraps. The brisk fire burns in an open range with three good ovens (the bottom one probably a sham) and a stout adjustable hook for the roasting-jack. There are tin canisters on the chimney-piece, a kettle-holder hanging from a nail, a stool, a broom, a fender, a shovel and tongs. Everything, in fact, for warmth and comfort, including a soft hearthrug which looks like sheepskin but is in fact (Ribby being what she is) a rabbitskin.

This delectable scene is observed from another angle when Ribby and Duchess are seated at the table with Duchess nervously exploring the interior of the pie. Here is another detail of cottage comfort: a thick hand-knitted shawl softening the wooden rails of Ribby's armchair, a very practical touch. And the handsome Edward VII 'coronation' tea-pot on the table which we have already seen on the hob, is undoubtedly one which Miss Potter herself had bought during her ramblings in Hawkshead or elsewhere; I recognized it more than thirty years ago on the chimney-piece at Troutbeck, one of her later and much more ambitious farm purchases.

One of the special delights of *The Pie and the Patty-pan* is the fidelity with which Beatrix Potter interprets cat and dog – but particularly cat – nature. This truth in the presentation of animal character dominates all her books during the magic years when inspiration was at its fertile and rapid best. Her animals, it is true, are to some extent interpreted in human terms: Ribby wears apron and shawl and goes shopping with a net purse and basket: but this method can be as veracious as translating a subject from one language into another. The technique is more than simply amusing to children, since it lays emphasis not only on the difference between man and animals but on the similarities between us. Thus, Tabitha Twitchit's reaction to the news that her cousin Ribby is having Duchess to tea (*after* their meeting in the village shop, of course – the manners of both cats are exemplary) is typical both of cats' dislike of dogs and of village snobbery. ' "A little *dog* indeed! Just as if there were no CATS in Sawrey! And a *pie* for afternoon tea! The very idea!" said Cousin Tabitha Twitchit.' A cat-and-dog friendship, however, was by no means an impossibility, as Beatrix Potter observed while staying at the blacksmith's. In a letter written from the Satterthwaites' to Fruing Warne she had included a message to his children: 'Tell Tonie there is a little dog called Midge in this cottage (cousin to Duchess), also a cat; and they are such friends they sit in the sun on the doorstep and the cat washes the dog's face and ruffle!'

Preferring cats to dogs as, on the whole, she did, Beatrix Potter seems nevertheless to have found a certain difficulty in drawing them to her liking. Norman Warne, too, had been critical of some of the cat drawings in the early stages. 'I don't feel perfectly satisfied with the eyes of the large head,' she had replied to one of his letters pointing out imperfections, 'but I think I can get it right. . .' It is impossible to fault any picture of either Ribby or Duchess in the finished version, and if Norman Warne had lived to see it even his perfectionism must have been satisfied. Only two tiny discrepancies seem to have escaped him – though no doubt he would have detected them at the proof stage. 'When Ribby had laid the table,' we are told, 'she took a jug and a blue and white dish, and went out down the field to the farm, to fetch milk and butter.' But in the picture the dish with the butter on it is *pink* and white. And in the scene in which Ribby is putting her uncooked pie into the oven, in 'a pie-dish with a pink rim', the crust of the pie is as brown as Ribby's paws, not at all the anaemic white of uncooked pastry. This, however, appears to be a fault in the colour-printing, since the pastry in the original is the colour of ivory. It is nevertheless the kind of minute divergence between text and picture for which Beatrix Potter had now to be doubly vigilant.

The little books in this period followed on one another's heels so fast, usually two a year and sometimes more, that one wonders in astonishment how so much good work could be accomplished as Miss Potter shuttled back and forth with her parents to the Lakes, and again, at Easter, between London and an endless succession of seaside lodgings. The answer is, in some cases, that the stories had been partly made up and experimental sketches roughed out a long time before, so that her drawing books and portfolios were full of ideas which she could brood on at leisure when the restless craving for a new book overtook her.

This was certainly the origin of her next story, *The Tale of Mr Jeremy Fisher*. As long ago as 1893, the day after she had written the Peter

Rabbit letter to Noël, she had made up another for his brother Eric. 'My dear Eric,' it began, 'Once upon a time there was a frog called Mr Jeremy Fisher, and he lived in a little house on the bank of a river . . .' This had been written from Dunkeld on the banks of the Tay, where Mr Potter was fond of taking his friends fishing and Beatrix and Bertram from an early age had been familiar with rowing-boats and fishing-tackle, with trout and perch and minnows and worms, and all the other hazards and excitements of angling and fly fishing. In her childhood and teens she had sometimes kept frogs as pets, observing their anatomy and behaviour and travelling with them on holidays. 'Poor little Punch died on the 11th', she had written in her journal when she was seventeen – 'green frog, had him five or six years. He has been on extensive journeys.'

In 1892 she had submitted a series of frog drawings to Nisters, a German firm of colour printers, in the hope that they might make them into a booklet, and had found herself engaged in a comic battle between their parsimony and her firmness. (Even in her twenties, it seems,

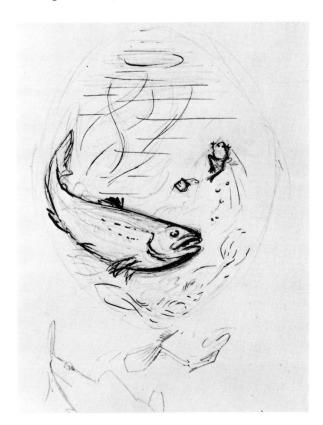

A rough sketch for the exciting scene when Jeremy Fisher escapes (leaving only his goloshes behind) from the enormous trout

Beatrix Potter was not without a certain shrewdness inherited from her cotton-spinning ancestors.) Nisters had first cautiously asked her how much she wanted for the drawings, warning her that it was out of their power to pay an exorbitant sum, 'as people do not want frogs now.' (Why not, one wonders?) Beatrix suggested twenty-five shillings for the ten drawings, but this apparently threw the firm into a panic, and they offered to return two, and pay a guinea for eight. This Miss Potter was 'not disposed to accept,' and their next inexplicable move was to offer a guinea for *nine* of the drawings – a proposal which she rejected by return of post, regretting that 'I am not willing to accept 21/– for 9, and I am of opinion that you had better return them without further discussion.' The tough line worked: Nisters replied with a cheque for 22/6, and the drawings were printed in a children's annual under the title *A Frog He Would a-Fishing Go*, supported by a set of lamentable verses.

Now, some twelve years later, her thoughts returned to the frog story, which she had already discussed with Norman – 'I should like to do Mr Jeremy Fisher too one day, and I think I could make something of him' – and she bought back the drawings from Nisters. 'They professed to have destroyed them,' she

(*above*) *An early sketch for* The Tale of Jeremy Fisher

(*right*) *Jeremy Fisher reading his newspaper, as printed in* The Tale, *and* (*above right*) *a rough sketch for the same subject*

He was quite pleased when he looked out and saw large drops of rain, splashing in the pond—

told Fruing Warne, 'until I bid them up to £6, when they were promptly "found".' They were early work and not particularly good, but the idea was attractive and she set about transferring Jeremy Fisher from the Tay to Esthwaite Water and exchanging his wooden boat for a lily leaf. The story is as simple as possible, but here again the imaginative parallel between frogs and human anglers in macintoshes, between newts and tortoises (both of which had been part of her nursery menagerie) and certain types of pompous elderly gentlemen, is eloquent. Beatrix Potter as a girl had often enough had to endure her father and his friends relating their fishing adventures, and the picture of Mr Jeremy Fisher retailing his mishap to Sir Isaac Newton is so rich in observation, both of amphibians and old gentlemen, that one is ever afterwards prone to confuse them in memory.

Jeremy Fisher's costume is impeccable; he is dressed throughout as a Regency buck and looks rather like Mr Pickwick – tights, pumps, starched collar and stock, bulging waistcoat. Sir Isaac Newton, as one would expect, has a waistcoat in black and gold and his attitudes, both standing and sitting, epitomize respectable Reform Club characters; while anyone who has seen Mr Ptolemy Tortoise knows exactly the appearance appropriate to an alderman. It is hard to understand why Graham Greene, in his memorable essay on Beatrix Potter, described *Jeremy Fisher* as the 'one failure' in this magical period of her best work. Perhaps he is not a fisherman?

It sold as well, at all events, as its predecessors, and Jeremy Fisher himself, long before he was translated into foreign languages or dazzled audiences as a star of ballet, became as familiar to three generations of children as any of Beatrix Potter's animal characters.

Jeremy Fisher was no sooner off her hands than she was snatching every available minute for another cat story, being now more than ever beguiled by Mrs Tabitha Twitchit and the kittens usually to be found scampering about Hill Top. She had managed to steal a few days in Sawrey for her own purposes, staying at the blacksmith's with her museum friend, Miss Woodward, sketching when she could bring herself to sit still, and when she could not, working hard to improve and plant the cottage garden. 'I went to see an old lady at Windermere,' she told Millie Warne, 'and impudently took a large basket and trowel with me. She had the most untidy overgrown garden I ever saw. I got nice things in handfuls without any shame, amongst others a bundle of lavender slips . . . Mrs Satterthwaite says stolen plants always grow ! . . . I have had something out of nearly every garden in the village.'

In the pictures which she drew for *The Tale of Tom Kitten* the garden of Hill Top is as full of blooms as a flower show. The porch is wreathed in clematis and the borders crowded with forget-me-nots, pansies, snapdragons, blackcurrants, and pinks. It was perhaps a vision of the garden as she hoped to make it, rather than as it was in Cannon's day. But the interior of the little house is faithfully exact, showing us precisely what it was like when the Cannon family had moved out and Miss Potter started to furnish it. The stone-flagged floors, oak panelling and deepset windows are as she found them, but there is a carpet and new blue-and-white curtains in Tabitha Twitchit's bedroom, a wall mirror and clock which were surely her own purchases. (Beatrix Potter had a passion for the old oak cupboards and chests which even then were too often ripped out of Lakeland farmhouses and cottages, and she rescued them from local furniture sales whenever possible.) And upstairs in the bedroom there is a solid canopied bed with red curtains, in which the three kittens are wildly demonstrating their right to be described as 'pickles'. 'Pickle' was a favourite word with Beatrix Potter. She had used it to describe her cousin, Caroline Hutton, whose free-thinking and suffragette opinions had been spiced with a trace of mischief, and now the kittens who scampered about the farmyard at Hill Top and romped in her flowerbeds seemed to her exactly the sort of characters who would find it impossible to behave well in 'elegant uncomfortable clothes' such as muslin pinafores and tuckers. The kitten she was using as a model was 'very young and pretty and a most fearful pickle . . . It is an exasperating model'; the book itself is dedicated 'To all PICKLES – especially to those that get up on my garden wall.'

The disaster which befalls the kittens in the story is the loss of their party clothes when, disobeying their mother's strict injunctions, they scramble over the wall to where Mr Drake Puddle-duck and the two duck-birds, Rebeccah and Jemima, stand staring at them in the lane. One of them has already put on the straw boater that Tom had lost. 'Mittens laughed so that she fell off the wall. Moppet and Tom descended after her; the pinafores and all the rest of Tom's clothes came off on the way down.' It was at this point, when he received the proposed script, that Fruing Warne, perhaps from a sense of propriety,

The porch at Hill Top

raised objections. He did not like '*all* the rest of Tom's clothes came off,' and suggested, as in better taste, '*nearly* all'. But this made Miss Potter laugh and she declined to alter it. ' "Nearly all" won't do! – because I have drawn Thomas already with *nothing*!' So the kittens remained unclad and their later pictures were completed at Lingholm, near Keswick, during the family holiday. 'I am wishing most heartily that I was back at Sawrey,' she wrote to Millie, 'but I suppose I shall scramble along here for a bit . . . I am up aloft with my drawing etc. in one of the attics. I thought there might be more air, but there is such a wind I think I shall be blown out . . . I miss the sheltered open air and the gardening.' The Puddle-ducks themselves could be dealt with in London, since there was a pond and ducks at Putney Park who served admirably as models. The Putney ducks appear in the last two pictures in the book, searching for Tom Kitten's clothes and demonstrating to all children why it is that ducks on ponds so often appear to be standing on their heads.

There was one special duck at Hill Top, however, whose maternal problems so appealed to Beatrix Potter's amused sympathy that she determined to give her a story of her own, one which would concentrate on the Hill Top farmyard and the nearby woods, and would also introduce a new and splendidly sinister character.

Ducks are notoriously bad at sitting on eggs and it was Mrs Cannon's practice to raise her broods of ducklings under a hen. Jemima Puddle-duck had made several attempts to establish a secret nest, but was always discovered, as we see in the picture where Ralph, the Cannons' little boy, is removing her eggs from under the rhubarb leaves in the kitchen garden. At this point 'Jemima Puddle-duck became quite desperate. She determined to make a nest right away from the farm,' so she (and also Beatrix Potter with her sketchbook) set off on a rapturous journey down the cart-road and over the hill that leads to the edge of the wood and a peaceful hazy view of Esthwaite Water.

This simple and flawless story, finally pruned down to what Graham Greene described as 'those brief, pregnant sentences which have slipped, like proverbs, into common speech', is really Beatrix Potter's poem about the farm itself, its human and animal characters, the northern summer beauty of its fields and woods. The idyllic landscape in which Jemima, wearing poke-bonnet and shawl, sets out to look for a secret nesting-place, is precisely what one sees, even today, after passing through the gate at the bottom of the farmyard. If you turn round, on the very spot where she stands at the end of the story, you look straight up the farmyard to the house. In more than seventy years it has hardly changed.

The dominant character in the story is, of course, not Jemima herself, but a fox, the 'elegantly dressed gentleman' with 'black prick ears and sandy coloured whiskers.' He was to become Beatrix Potter's favourite villain, and from the moment when we see him, seated among the foxgloves and looking intently at Jemima over his newspaper, we begin to absorb the essentials of foxy character. He is handsome, faultlessly dressed, extremely clever. His manners are impeccable. As he leads poor simple Jemima to the security of his 'very retired, dismal-looking house amongst the foxgloves', we recognize in him the epitome of the experienced, crafty, ruthless sporting gentleman. Jemima, like little Red Riding Hood, is an innocent. The fact that the shed is full of feathers does not rouse her suspicion, for 'it was comfortable and very soft . . . and she made a nest without any trouble at all.' The fox behaves in the most considerate and chivalrous manner. 'He was so polite, that he seemed almost sorry to let Jemima go home for the night. He promised to take great care of her nest until she came back again next day. He said he loved eggs and ducklings; he should be proud to see a fine nestful in his woodshed.' But when the clutch is almost complete and he counts the eggs like a miser in Jemima's absence, we see him for what he is – a fox without disguise, beautiful in his wild pelt.

An early sketch for a scene in The Tale of Jemima Puddle-Duck

Jemima's story, as Beatrix Potter was fond of pointing out, is really
Little Red Riding Hood retold, and in following this direct and un-
sentimental pattern she was influenced by her own love of fairy tales.
Children are not generally squeamish when it comes to being slain by
giants or eaten by ogres; they take such things in their imaginative
stride, and one of the origins of the fairy tale may well have been the
necessity of teaching children to be careful. The results of too great
innocence or rashness, in the classic fairy tales as in Beatrix Potter's
stories, are much the same. They point no moral, save that the helpless
and the simple, if they are not wary, may make a meal for somebody
else – a truism fully as applicable in the modern world as in the jungle.
Red Riding Hood had always been one of Beatrix Potter's favourite
myths, and a few years after the publication of *Jemima Puddle-Duck* she
wrote her own version, following Perrault's grim seventeenth-century
fable, in which both Red Riding Hood and her grandmother are eaten
by the wolf. This is how it ends – a surprise, perhaps, for anyone who
thinks of Beatrix Potter as either squeamish or sentimental:

> 'What big strong hairy arms you have got, Granny!' said Red Riding
> Hood.
> 'The better to hug you, my dear!'
> 'What big hairy ears under your night-cap!'
> 'The better to hear you, little Grand-daughter!'
> 'But Granny – your eyes have turned yellow!'
> 'The better to see you, my pretty!'
> 'But Granny, Granny, what big white teeth – '
> 'And that' [wrote Beatrix Potter] 'was the end of little Red Riding
> Hood.'

It was not until the late 1860s that versions of this fairy tale had appeared
with a happy ending, which must have calmed the fears of a great many
nurseries. Latter-day children are willing to be harrowed by suspense,
but on the whole they prefer adventures to end comfortably, and it
would have been unbearable to Ralph and Betsy Cannon, to whom
Jemima Puddle-Duck was dedicated, if that simple person were last seen
in the sinister woodshed as a mess of blood and feathers. So Kep, the
noble Hill Top collie, becomes suspicious, passing the word to two fox-
hound puppies 'out at walk with the butcher', so that the villain is
pursued and presumably destroyed, while Jemima is rescued with all

the dashing speed and action of a wild-west movie. The eggs are lost, of course, but she is allowed to sit on her next brood and manages to hatch four, a poor result by Mrs Cannon's standard. 'Jemima Puddle-duck said that it was because of her nerves,' Beatrix Potter tells us; 'but she had always been a bad sitter.'

Study of the gentleman with sandy whiskers

It is perhaps a fitting last word to this story that after Beatrix Potter's death, some thirty-six years after her loving delineation of the country about Hill Top, her ashes were scattered in the field at the edge of Jemima's wood, looking back to Sawrey on the one side and on the other over Esthwaite Water.

Miss Potter's pleasure in improving the interior of the farmhouse was enhanced by the fact that she was using it as the setting for the book which was to become her masterpiece. The Cannons were settled in the small new wing; the spacious kitchen and dairy and little parlour, the stairs and landing and upstairs rooms, even the attics, were her own. Though modest in size and of unprepossessing exterior the house had been well and solidly built in the seventeenth century with thick walls, leaded windows, stone floors, good oak panelling and a handsome staircase with carved balusters. With a few refinements it could be made into the sort of house that she loved best.

A study of Kep, the Hill Top sheep-dog

But there was a problem – rats, who for decades, perhaps centuries, had used underground tunnels and passages through the walls and behind skirtings, living in a secret labyrinth from which they carried out skilful raids all over the farm. Beatrix Potter had long known about the Cannons' fruitless efforts to exterminate them, and had made the rats the focus of a story written for Winifred Warne, the little girl who had the doll's house. This early version had been illustrated with two watercolours and a number of pen-and-ink drawings in sepia, and she was now busy on a set of larger watercolours, since Warnes had agreed to give the book the benefit of the larger format.

'She set off on a fine spring afternoon along the cart-road
that leads over the hill' – the field at the edge of Jemima's wood where
Beatrix Potter's ashes were eventually scattered.

Everything about the story appealed to her and gave her pleasure. Hill Top itself would be celebrated in fine detail, including a sooty ascent of the kitchen chimney and a ravishing view of stone walls, slate tiles and apple-blossom that one saw if one climbed to the roof. The Hill Top cats, led by that 'pickle', Tom, would be among the characters. 'I think that some day,' she had written towards the end of their adventure with the Puddle-ducks, 'I shall have to make another, larger book, to tell you more about Tom Kitten!' Now he was to have an

Sketch for the kitchen stove in The Tale of Samuel Whiskers
(*originally* The Roly-Poly Pudding)

even more terrifying experience than Jemima Puddle-duck's, and she did not shrink from introducing an element of agonizing horror, which was to make *The Roly-Poly Pudding* the finest in that group of stories which Graham Greene, with affectionate mockery, calls her 'great near-tragedies'.

For this sinister element she had, of course, the rats. 'I have had an amusing afternoon thoroughly exploring the house,' she wrote to Millie Warne. 'It really is delightful – if the rats could be stopped out! There is one wall four feet thick with a staircase inside it. I never saw such a place for hide and seek and funny cupboards and closets.' And later, visiting the house daily to organize her practical improvements: 'The rats have come back in great force; two big ones were trapped in the shed here, besides turning out a nest of eight baby rats in the cucumber frame opposite the door. They are getting at the corn at the farm. Mrs Cannon calmly announced that she should get four or five cats!' And a week later, 'The cats have not arrived yet, but Mrs Cannon has seen a rat sitting up eating its dinner under the kitchen table in the middle of the afternoon. We are putting zinc on the bottoms of the doors – that and cement skirtings will puzzle them.'

Yet, for all their menace and destruction, Beatrix Potter had a certain sympathy with the rascals. If only they would keep out of Hill Top she would have been happy to think of them prospering somewhere else. She had long ago kept a pet white rat of her own, and remembered his accomplishments and failings. 'Poor Sammy! White rats are not very long lived; and he was always wanting to be petted in his declining months – but not everybody liked him . . . He carried a curious collection of stolen articles to his box. I remember my Aunt providing a hard-boiled egg, and watching the rolling of the egg along a passage . . .' Remembering Sammy, she had everything she needed to portray that resourceful and unscrupulous pilferer, Mr Samuel Whiskers.

The story plunges at once into an atmosphere of suspense. Mrs Tabitha Twitchit has decided to imprison her kittens in a cupboard on baking day, to keep them out of mischief; but she cannot find Tom. As she searches, we are shown around Hill Top in luxurious detail. 'She went right upstairs and looked into the attics, but she could not find him anywhere. It was an old, old house, full of cupboards and passages. Some of the walls were four feet thick, and there used to be queer noises inside them, as if there might be a little secret staircase. Certainly there were odd little jagged doorways in the wainscot, and things disappeared

'On baking day she determined to shut them up in a cupboard'

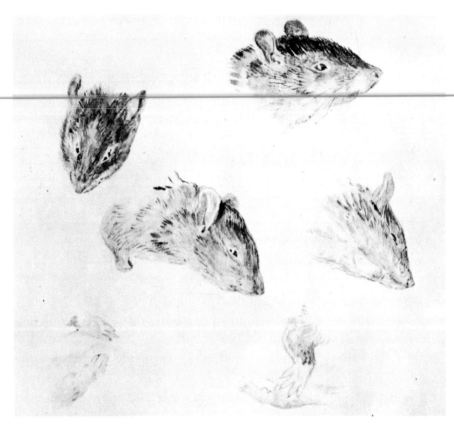

Studies of rats' heads done in preparation for Samuel Whiskers

at night – especially cheese and bacon. Mrs Tabitha became more and more distracted, and mewed dreadfully.' We see her on the staircase, standing before Miss Potter's new plum-coloured curtains, and when Cousin Ribby calls to borrow some yeast (it is baking day, remember) we are shown the heavy front-door and a glimpse of the garden framing one of the most enchanting cat-pictures ever painted. Together they search the attics and the great clothes-chest, but to no avail; the thought of the rats that infest the house becomes more ominous. There is a 'curious roly-poly noise under the attic floor'; Moppet, hiding in a flour-barrel, has seen 'an old woman rat' filching dough from the crock in the kitchen, while Mittens, concealed in the dairy, has seen an old man rat – 'a dreadful 'normous big rat, mother' – stealing a pat of butter and a rolling-pin. Our apprehensions become unbearable, and we are quickly switched, with the aid of a wonderfully exact kitchen picture, to what was actually happening to Tom Kitten.

(right) A slight variant of the illustration of Tabitha Twitchit searching for Tom Kitten

(left) Tom Kitten looking for a hiding place up the chimney. The kitchen range has changed slightly from that in the sketch on page 160

'A dreadful 'normous big rat'. Rough sketch for the
watercolour in The Tale of Samuel Whiskers

Not wanting to be shut up in a cupboard he had decided to take refuge in the chimney, and there, wandering in soot and darkness and falling through a hole into the lair of the predatory rat who inhabits the place, he is captured, tied and encased in dough as a preliminary to boiling him as a pudding. The text is terse and ironic, the pictures are beautiful and frightening – Tom Kitten bound, mewing and helpless under the rafters, then wriggling and spitting while Samuel Whiskers and his wife Anna Maria knead him into pudding shape with the rolling-pin.

But help is at hand. John Joiner the practical carpenter dog has been summoned from the village, a plank has been lifted in the attic, Tom Kitten is rescued and the rats have fled with their possessions ('and other people's') to Farmer Potatoes' barn. The children of Sawrey and their parents too would have recognized every detail of the final pictures, for

Tom Kitten 'fell head over heels in the dark, down a hole, and landed
on a heap of very dirty rags.' Another sketch for a watercolour in the book

The two rats 'sat staring at him with their mouths open.'

Farmer Potatoes was in reality Farmer Postlethwaite, a near neighbour, whom Beatrix Potter photographed for her purpose, and there is even a distant portrait of Miss Potter herself at the end of the village, staring after the rats as they scamper to safety with their loot piled on a wheelbarrow. One of the last pictures in the book is of Tabitha Twitchit comfortably dozing by the kitchen fire, her paws on her lap and her knitting fallen on the hearthrug. Hill Top is finally at peace.

The Roly-Poly Pudding was issued in smaller numbers than its predecessors, since Warnes (and perhaps Miss Potter too) argued that a price of half-a-crown was bound to restrict the sales of the large format. After eight years of steady popularity the title was changed to *The Tale of Samuel Whiskers* and the book reissued in the small size to match *Peter Rabbit* and the rest, which was a pity. The illustrations are so

Samuel Whiskers collects the rolling-pin
'pushing it in front of him . . . like a brewer's man trundling a barrel.'

(right) The frontispiece
The Roly-Poly
Pudding, of which the
original sketch is slightly
damaged, and (left) a rough
watercolour sketch of it

(left) The watercolour
sketch and (right) the
final printed illustration
of the rolling-pin
episode

They could not find anything, but they both thought that they heard a slight roley poley noise under the attic floor. And once they heard a door bang, and somebody scuttered down stairs—

"Yes, it is infested with rats," said Tabitha tearfully. "I caught 7 young ones out of one hole in the back kitchen and we had them for dinner. And once I saw the old father rat, an enormous old rat, Cousin Ribby; I was just going to jump upon him when he showed his yellow teeth at me, and whisked down the hole."

A page of the original manuscript, with line drawings, for Samuel Whiskers

exceptionally fine that one would have thought the large format worth continuing as well as the small, for the sake of Hill Top and the devotees of Tom Kitten and Samuel Whiskers.

As to that self-indulgent and totally undefeatable character, it seems that he reappeared at Hill Top, though only spasmodically, as soon as the book was out. 'I am glad to tell you,' Beatrix Potter wrote in a letter to a little friend, 'he is still living at Farmer Potatoes'. He only comes up now and then to Hill Top Farm. He never came near the place for months . . . but one evening there was a visit from Mr Whiskers! I was sitting very quiet before the fire . . . reading a book, and I heard some-one pitter-patter along the passage . . . I thought it was the puppy or the kitten, so I took no notice. But next morning we discovered that Mr Whiskers had been in the house! We could not find him anywhere, so we think he had got in – and out again – by squeezing under a door. He had stolen the very oddest thing! There is a sort of large cupboard or closet where I do my photographing; it is papered inside with rather a pretty green and gold paper, and Samuel had torn off strips of paper all round the closet as high as he could reach, and I think *she* must have wanted to paper her best sitting-room. I only wonder she did not take the paste-brush, which was on a shelf in the closet. Perhaps she intended coming back for the brush next night. If she did, she was disappointed, for I asked John Joiner to make a heavy hard plank of wood to fit into the opening under the door; and it seems to keep out Mr and Mrs Whiskers.'

Samuel Whiskers and his wife on the run

All the same, her sympathy for that 'persecuted (but irrepressible) race' remained. The book was dedicated to her old white rat Sammy – 'an affectionate little friend and most accomplished thief'– and on the reverse of the title-page of *The Roly-Poly Pudding* is the coat of arms granted to Samuel Whiskers, with the appropriate motto, 'Resurgam' – 'I shall return'.

As indeed he did, if we may judge from a correspondence written several years later. Here are the relevant letters, long preserved in a child's miniature post-bag:

To Samuel Rat, High Barn.

Sir,

I hereby give you one day's notice to quit my barn and stables and byre, with your wife, children and grandchildren and great-grand-children to the latest generation.

signed: William Potatoes, farmer
witness: Gilbert Cat and John Stoat-Ferret

Farmer Potatoes, The Priddings.

Sir,

I have opened a letter addressed to one Samuel Rat. If Samuel Rat means me, I inform you I shall *not go*, and you can't turn us out.

Yrs. etc.
Samuel Whiskers.

Mr Obadiah Rat, Barley Mill.

Dear Friend Obadiah,

Expect us – bag and baggage – at 9 o'clock in the morning. Am sorry to come upon you suddenly; but my landlord William Potatoes has given me one day's notice to quit. I am of opinion that it is not legal & I could sit till Candlemas because the notice is not addressed to me in my proper surname. *I* would stand up to William Potatoes, but my wife will not face John Stoat-Ferret, so we have decided on a midnight flitting as it is full-moon. I think there are 96 of us, but am not certain. Had it been the May-day term we could have gone to the Field Drains, but it is out of question at this season. Trusting that the meal bags are full.

Yr. obliged friend,
Samuel Whiskers.

'As for Farmer Potatoes he has been driven nearly distracted. There are rats, and rats, and rats in his barn.'

The real Farmer Potatoes – Farmer Postlethwaite of Sawrey. On the back of the original photograph is written, 'This is my father, Farmer Potatoes, and my sister Ruth and I taken outside Buckleyeat, Sawrey. Then Mary Postlethwaite, now Mary Fleming, Whinfell, Sawrey'.

8
THE PATH TO
CASTLE COTTAGE

Beatrix Potter's life was now divided into three parts, and in trying to fit them together she often found herself as 'distracted' as Tabitha Twitchit. First and foremost were the affairs of Hill Top: John Cannon was increasing the herd of Galloways and the farm had already earned an enviable reputation for pigs. She was snatching every opportunity of spending days or weeks at Sawrey by herself, describing herself as 'a sort of self-contained independent female farmer', taking part in village affairs, judging trussed poultry at agricultural shows and standing for election to local committees. 'I have been much driven with canvassing and squabbles,' she wrote to Harold Warne, 'and collecting proxies to squash my opponent.' But even more important was 'the question of buying a pedigree bull calf and the exasperatingly wet weather – the lower fields are strewn with the potatoes of my next-door neighbour, a very casual farmer; he must have had tons washed out . . . The hay has got soaked again.'

It was difficult to find time for sketching, photographing, painting or working out possible themes for new stories, but all these activities were essential to her life at Hill Top, since it was the income from her little books which made it possible. She was producing them at the rate of two a year and their fame had spread to many parts of the world, involving her in correspondence with children whom she had never seen and who wrote to her from places as remote as America or New Zealand. Her publishers were eager for more, so her own work had to be fitted in with a busy lambing-time, singling the turnips, getting in hay or whatever was the farmer's most pressing need at the moment.

As well as this, of course, there was the inevitable round of holidays and visits with her parents to furnished houses, to rented apartments, to seaside hotels and the country estates of their relations, all now complicated by the fact that Mr and Mrs Potter were growing old and her father's health was rapidly deteriorating. 'I think I shall only stay over the weekend to see if my father is all right after the journey,' she wrote after a difficult spell with them at Windermere, 'and then I will go to

Sawrey – for a rest!' She had been travelling to Hill Top on every possible occasion by the local coach, and this had been both tiring and time-consuming. 'I never had such an exhausting summer . . . The farm has done very well, but neighbours have suffered much with the hay . . . I have done no sketching, partly weather and partly waste of time and energy on the road . . . the coach has run very irregularly . . . three hours per day makes a hole in the 24 hours!'

Yet in spite of all difficulties her imagination was delightedly at work, and a family visit to her Uncle Burton at Gwaynynog was turned to good account for the latest rabbit adventure she was devising – *The Tale of the Flopsy Bunnies*. Peter Rabbit and his relations had by now proved so universally popular and profitable that it was useless for their author to protest that she was tired of doing rabbits. It was Peter's name, in fact, rather than Beatrix Potter's, that had become famous; he was now translated into French and German, pirated editions had appeared in America, and the German toy manufacturers, very much to the injury of the English doll trade, were flooding the market with cheap stuffed Peter Rabbits and Benjamin Bunnies. So, giving up her protests and returning to 'those wearisome rabbits' for whom she still felt a personal affection, she made use of the beautiful walled garden at Gwaynynog, with its espalier apple trees and apricots on the walls, and its deep ditch into which Mr McGregor threw rotten vegetables together with his worn-out boots and oily lawn-mowings.

The story, dedicated to 'All little friends of Mr McGregor and Peter and Benjamin', is slightly longer and more sophisticated than the earlier rabbit stories. It contains twenty-five exquisite watercolours of garden scenes and rabbit activities, some of them with glimpses of Mr and Mrs McGregor, who have now been a menace to three generations of Peter's family. Benjamin Bunny is grown-up and married to his cousin Flopsy, with a large family, 'and they were very improvident and cheerful.' Peter Rabbit and his mother keep a nursery garden. The noticeboard above their fence reads: 'Peter Rabbit and Mother, Florists. Gardens neatly razed. Borders devastated by the Night or Year.' (This picture had to be redrawn after the third printing, *without* the noticeboard, because of the problems involved in foreign translation.)

Beatrix Potter abandons her usual 'Once upon a time', of which she was rather tired, and indulges her fondness for the occasional impressive word – a taste which she believed to be shared by most children. 'It is

The frontispiece to The Tale of the Flopsy Bunnies *shows Mr McGregor walking through a garden which is evidently a re-creation of the beautiful walled garden at Gwaynynog.*

'Mrs Flopsy Bunny came across the field. She looked suspiciously at the sack and wondered where everybody was.'

said that the effect of eating too much lettuce is "soporific". *I* have never felt sleepy after eating lettuces; but then *I* am not a rabbit. They certainly had a very soporific effect upon the Flopsy Bunnies.'

Benjamin Bunny and his children, when their larder is empty, stuff themselves with overgrown lettuces on Mr McGregor's rubbish-heap and fall asleep in the pile of lawn-mowings, where the crafty old gardener presently finds them. Benjamin is hidden under a paper bag, but the sleeping little ones are collected into a sack for Mr McGregor's supper and left on the wall while he puts away his mowing-machine. It is at this point that Mrs Flopsy Bunny, who had remained at home, comes slowly across the field in her blue pinafore, a solitary figure in one of Beatrix Potter's most emotionally evocative landscapes. 'She looked suspiciously at the sack and wondered where everybody was?' It is impossible to say exactly how it is done, but the back view of the mother rabbit is so eloquent of anxiety and, at the same time, caution, that one would know her thoughts even without the text.

Help, mercifully, is at hand in the person of a character whom we now meet for the first time, Mrs Thomasina Tittlemouse, who was 'a resourceful person' and nibbles a hole in the sack so that the little rabbits can be rescued and the sack refilled with decaying vegetable marrows and rotten turnips. The story, in fact, follows the basic pattern of so many fairy tales, whose primitive origins lie in the harsh law of nature – everyone is a potential meal for somebody else, unless he is very careful. With the Flopsy Bunnies as with the fairy tale, a happy ending means that the trick is turned on the aggressor, so Mr and Mrs McGregor become angry and quarrelsome when they find he has been fooled, and the rabbit family scurry away out of the Gwaynynog garden to the safety of their burrow. Thomasina Tittlemouse, looking ravishingly pretty in the final picture, is rewarded the following Christmas with 'enough rabbit wool to make herself a cloak and a hood, and a handsome muff and a pair of warm mittens.'

Such a co-operative, tidy and practical little mouse – not a house-mouse this time but 'a wood-mouse with a long tail' – was too attractive a heroine to be dismissed, so by the end of 1909 Beatrix Potter had written out her story in an exercise book, with twenty-one pages of text and eight watercolours, as a New Year present for Harold Warne's little daughter Nellie. This, of course, was the preliminary version of a new book which would appear some six months later, improved in text and with twenty-six colour pictures which take one straight down a tidy mouse-hole 'in a bank under a hedge', where the careful little housewife, 'a most terribly tidy particular little mouse, always sweeping and dusting the soft sandy floors' has exasperating problems with unwanted visitors. (It is odd, by the way, since the names of so many of Beatrix Potter's characters have passed into our language, that it is Mrs Tiggy-winkle's name which is usually applied – in a commendatory sense, of course – to the super-punctilious housewife, whereas it should really be Mrs Tittlemouse's. The only reason I can suggest is that Mrs Tiggy-winkle, who was such an excellent laundress but a bit of a muddler, had already enjoyed five years of nursery fame before Mrs Tittlemouse made her modest bow, and Tiggy had already been cast for the role of domestic perfectionist.)

Mrs Tittlemouse's store-rooms are full, her nut-cellars and seed-cellars in good order, her bedroom and sandy passages clean and tidy. She appears to have no family and therefore, presumably, few problems; but this is not the case; she is invaded from every quarter by intruders. Beetles leave dirty footmarks, ladybirds wander in her clean passages, spiders come in from the rain, butterflies lick her sugar, humble-bees make a nest with dry moss in one of her storerooms, and – worst of all – Mr Jackson, the invasive toad, attracted by the smell of honey, is found amiably sitting by her fireside, waiting to be fed. Toads *are* amiable creatures, as Beatrix Potter well knew, and seem often unperturbed when discovered in unlikely places. (There was one who for several years came occasionally into my house during the hot weather and sat placidly on the stone floor behind the umbrella-stand.) Beatrix had kept her own pet toad for more than a year (before he jumped off the window-sill) when she was seventeen, and had studied his feeding habits. It may have been his interest in a nursery tea-tray that led to the discovery or theory that toads like honey, or – perhaps more likely – her youthful researches in the Natural History Museum could have taught her that they are, indeed, partial to most insects, including humble-bees, and will invade the moss-lined burrow (usually the deserted run of a mouse or shrew) in which the humble-bee lays her eggs and builds a small honeycomb to support her imminent family.

The toad is very different from Jeremy Fisher. He moves ponderously, is not at all afraid of the bees and pulls out their nest with methodical greed, leaving Mrs Tittlemouse to clear up the mess of moss, mud, thistledown and beeswax. Like her creator, however, Thomasina is nothing if not practical. First she reduces the size of her front door, making it too small for Mr Jackson: then, after a good night's sleep, she begins a restorative spring-cleaning which lasts a fortnight. 'She swept, and scrubbed, and dusted; and she rubbed up the furniture with beeswax, and polished her little tin spoons.' To all this activity, as to the domestic character of the little mouse herself, Beatrix Potter responded with a deep and instinctive sympathy. The spring-cleaning of the mouse-hole has the same feeling as the refurnishing and polishing of Hill Top, where she had already installed a handsome oak dresser, a grandfather clock, her grandmother's copper warming-pan and a quantity of old teapots and plates and other treasures. When the nest is at last 'all beautifully neat and clean' Mrs Tittlemouse gives a celebratory party to five other little mice, with Mr Jackson kept out but allowed a glass of honey-dew passed through the window. The two final pictures, of the party, have their charm, but it is the two preceding ones – Mrs Tittlemouse polishing her spoons and falling asleep exhausted in her rocking-chair by the fire, that remain permanently in the memory. The exquisite drawing and colour, combined with an intimate understanding both of female wood-mouse nature and its human counterpart, are as moving and memorable to a grown-up as to a child. That is one of the secrets of Beatrix Potter's art in this best period, when she still retained the vision of childhood but had become aware of her mature character in its own right.

She was now in her mid-forties; the semi-independence which her own success and the ownership of Hill Top had brought her was producing an impressive development of personality. She was still the dutiful and respectful daughter she had always been, but the wearisome attendance on her parents' peregrinations was endured with increasing impatience, expressed from time to time to her cousin Caroline (now married to the Laird of Ulva and living on a small island off the coast of Mull), or to Millie Warne. Nowhere, however, is her new sense of maturity and self-confidence more apparent than in her letters to her publishers. With the death of Norman she had lost the one influence with whose perception and judgment she could always agree. With Harold Warne it was different. She found his judgments sometimes puritanical and timid, and did not hesitate to say so. (Though herself a 'total abstainer'

Mrs Tittlemouse went on her way
to a distant storeroom to fetch
cherry stones and thistle down seed
for dinner.
All along the passage she sniffed
and looked at the floor.

"I smell the smell of honey,
is it the cowslips in the hedge?
I am sure I can see the marks
of little dirty feet!"

*On this and the opposite page
are reproduced pages of manuscript
and watercolour sketches for*
The Tale of Mrs Tittlemouse,
*inscribed on the fly-leaf 'For Nellie,
with love and best wishes for
a Happy New Year, Jan. 1, 1910'.
Nellie was Nellie Warne.*

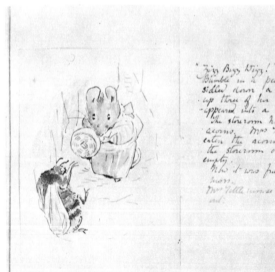

"Zizz Bizz Wizz!" replied Babbitty
Bumble in a peevish squeak; she
sidled down a passage holding
up three of her legs, and disappeared into a storeroom.
The storeroom had been used for
acorns. Mrs Tittlemouse had
eaten the acorns before Christmas;
the storeroom ought to have been
empty.
Now it was full of untidy dry
moss.
Mrs Tittlemouse began to pull it
out.

"How do you do Mr Jackson?
Very bad! you have got very
wet!"
"Thank ye thank ye thank you!
Mrs Tittlemouse! I'll sit awhile
and dry myself" said Mr Jackson.

Mrs Tittlemouse went round
with a mop!

Mr Jackson sat and smiled
and the water dropped off his
coat tails.

On this page are two sketches
of the immortal Mr Jackson,
in The Tale of Mrs Tittlemouse.
These were obviously the original
drawings for The Tale, but
certain slight changes were made
in the finished drawings
for the book.

Then she offered him thistledown
seed—
"Tiddly, widdly widdly! Pouf,
pouff, puff!" said Mr Jackson,
and he blew the thistledown all
over the parlour.

(What extraordinary manners!)
thought the indignant Mrs
Tittlemouse.

Then she offered him beech-nuts—
"Thank you, thank you, thank
you, Mrs Tittlemouse! now what
I really—really should like
—would be a little dish of
honey!"

she had never quite got over his deletion of the rollicking rats in *The Tailor of Gloucester*.) Herself very much a perfectionist, his criticisms sometimes struck her as excessive. 'I am agreeably surprised with the proofs, following your letter,' she wrote in the summer of 1909, when *Ginger and Pickles* was in progress. 'I really think – if not uncivil to say so – you get things on your nerves at this time of year; these blocks are quite good!' Then there was the question of propriety. The wood-lice hiding in Mrs Tittlemouse's plate-rack, for instance, had to be changed to 'creepy-crawly people' because of the undesirability of the word 'lice' in a book for children. This prompted her to ask him, when she was working on the text of *Mr Tod*, 'whether you (or Mrs Grundy) object to the name of Bull Banks? One thinks nothing about bulls and tups in the farming world, but after you objected to cigars it occurred to me to wonder.' (He had hesitated over Tommy Brock smoking a 'cabbage-leaf cigar' as, presumably, too rakish, but Miss Potter had insisted.) He had been nervous, too, over the morality of the book's theme, and had criticized her opening paragraph, in which she had candidly proposed to 'make a story about two disagreeable people'. 'I cannot think what you are driving at,' she wrote in exasperation. 'If it were not impertinent to lecture one's publisher – you are a great deal too much afraid of the public, for whom I have never cared one tuppenny button. I am *sure* that it is that attitude of mind which has enabled me to keep up the series. Most people, after one success, are so cringingly afraid of doing less well that they rub all the edge off their subsequent work. I have always thought the opening paragraph distinctly *good*, because it gets away from "once upon a time".' And when the possibility of manufacturing Peter Rabbit dolls was being discussed, 'I must ask you *not to make any arrangements* without letting me know. I am *seriously provoked* about things being in such a muddle.'

Nevertheless, she got on so well with the Warne family as a whole that these occasional outbursts did no more than ruffle the surface. She had become an extremely valuable property to her publisher, and he must often have regretted her growing passion for farming and land-ownership, since it frequently got in the way of creative work and left her exhausted. For the present, however, there was no sign of any falling-off, and so long as she could place the scenes of her stories in Sawrey the work was pure pleasure.

In the autumn of 1908 she had written and sketchily illustrated a new story, *Ginger and Pickles*, as a Christmas present for Harold Warne's little girl, Louie. This was now Beatrix Potter's professional method – to write out the story in an exercise book, do one or two watercolours and a number of pen-and-ink sketches which could be pasted in, inscribe the result as a present and 'try it out on the children'.

The inspiration of *Ginger and Pickles* was the village shop in Smithy Lane, originally kept by John Taylor the Sawrey joiner and wheelwright, and now, since he was old and bedridden, by his wife and middle-aged daughter. It was the focus of village life, as much a centre for meetings and gossip as the Tower Bank Arms. Everybody bought their tea and candles there, their bacon and biscuits, bars of yellow soap and red cotton spotted handkerchiefs. The small window displayed jars of barley-sugar and boxes of peppermint rock. 'In fact,' as Beatrix Potter wrote in her story, 'although it was such a small shop it sold nearly everything – except a few things that you want in a hurry – like bootlaces, hair-pins and mutton chops.' (Alas, the shop has long since disappeared, though the original house still stands and can be identified by a few details, such as the old meat-hooks hanging from the ceiling of the back room. Beatrix Potter would have been sad if she could have foreseen the defeat of the village shop everywhere in our own time, fleeing before the heavy artillery of the supermarket.)

The shop run by Ginger and Pickles, a tom-cat and a terrier, runs into difficulties because of their obliging but unwise system of giving credit. 'Now the meaning of "credit",' Beatrix Potter informs her young readers, 'is this – when a customer buys a bar of soap, instead of the customer pulling out a purse and paying for it – she says she will pay another time. And Pickles makes a low bow and says, "With pleasure, Madam", and it is written down in a book. The customers come again and again and buy quantities, in spite of being afraid of Ginger and Pickles.' The rabbits do all their shopping there, trying to disregard the dog behind the counter; mice, too, are regular customers, notwithstanding the alert presence of the cat. 'Ginger usually requested Pickles to serve them, because he said it made his mouth water. "I cannot bear," said he, "to see them going out at the door carrying their little parcels." '

Once the making of the book was in progress and it became known in the village that it was to be about Sawrey, the neighbours began to show a competitive spirit. The book had been 'causing amusement', she wrote to Millie Warne when at last she had finished it. 'It has got a

Two of seventeen sketches in sepia ink for the illustrations to The Tale of Ginger and Pickles. These sketches, mounted in an exercise book, were given to Louie Warne, inscribed 'With love from Auntie Beatrix. Christmas 1908'. They are different from, and rather more free than, the illustrations that finally appeared in the book.

good many views which can be recognized in the village, which is what they like; they are all jealous of each other's houses and cats getting into a book.' Understandably anxious to be represented was old John Taylor, the shop's owner, and since it seemed likely that he had not long to live Beatrix Potter decided to dedicate the book to him, instead of to Louie Warne, if her father had no objection. 'Old John,' she wrote many years later, 'was a sweet gentle old man, failed in his legs, so he kept to his bed, but was the head of the family . . . He professed to be jealous because I had put his son in a book as John Joiner. When I saw old John, who was very humorous and jokey, I asked him how I could put him – old John – in a book if he insisted on living in bed? So a week afterwards, enclosed with an account, there came a scrap of paper – "John Taylor's compliments and thinks he might pass for a dormouse." '

The finished copy was therefore sent to Warnes 'DEDICATED with very kind regards to old Mr John Taylor, who "thinks he might pass as a dormouse!" (three years in bed and never a grumble!)'. 'I do not know what you will say to this dedication,' she wrote to Harold Warne. 'In a way – it ought to be Louie's book, but she can look forward. I sometimes think poor old John Taylor is keeping alive to see this one printed. I should rather like to put his name in if you don't object?' And a few weeks later, 'Old "John Dormouse" was given up last Wednesday, but is now extremely lively, smoking his pipe in bed. Let me have a copy for him as soon as there is one to spare and ready.' The old man, in fact, did not live to see the book published, but his acknowledged part in the *Ginger and Pickles* drama was undoubtedly the most cheering interest of his final days.

For her other village friends, particularly the children, Beatrix Potter introduced a number of already popular characters. The dolls which Norman Warne had bought for her in Seven Dials are remembered on the first page, since 'Lucinda and Jane Doll-cook always bought their groceries at Ginger and Pickles.' Peter Rabbit and his relations crowd the shop, while Samuel Whiskers surveys the counter, running up 'a bill as long as his tail', and Jeremy Fisher tries on a pair of goloshes. Mrs Tiggy-winkle is there buying soap, as one would expect, and there is a glimpse of Anna Maria pocketing cream crackers and a close view of Jemima Puddle-duck, Squirrel Nutkin and various other small characters busily pilfering or gossiping outside the shop. Sally Henny Penny,

who takes over the business when Ginger and Pickles have ruined themselves and gone off to other occupations, is suitably attired in a jet-
trimmed mantle and bonnet remarkably like Mrs Potter's. Old John
Taylor and his daughter are brought in at the end, receiving complaints
from some hard-working tailor-mice about the quality of their candles.
The interior of the shop throughout is portrayed in loving detail: one
can almost smell the groceries. And the endpapers – a change from her
usual ones since *Ginger and Pickles* was published in the large format –
give us an enchanting vision of what probably went on in the shop after
closing hours. In the first pair a mouse has fallen into an empty sweet-
jar and is rescued by resourceful mates with a ball of string; in the
second, the mice have fun swinging on the scales and Jeremy Fisher
and his friends weigh themselves on the same apparatus, gesticulating
and piscatorially reminiscing.

In the summer of 1909, a few months before *Ginger and Pickles* was
published, Beatrix Potter had bought Castle Farm, a small property only
a few hundred yards from Hill Top, on the outskirts of Near Sawrey.
The fields of the two farms could be conveniently joined, and there was
a path leading across from one to the other. She was now well on her
way to owning half the village. This purchase had been made through
a firm of Hawkshead and Ambleside solicitors, W. Heelis and Sons, an
old-established family business which for two generations had handled
the property transfers of the district; and the partner who dealt personally with Miss Potter and drew up the contract for her was Mr William
Heelis, a quiet, tall, leisurely man a few years younger than herself, who
had been born and educated at Appleby and had hardly ever been outside his native Lake District. William Heelis had known all the local
farmers and landowners since he was a boy and was able to give her
sound advice during the purchase, and later, when she was struggling
with the problems of laying on a water supply to the new property, his
experience was invaluable. He sympathized with her passion for Sawrey
and for the farming life, while she, for her part, understood and appreciated his country tastes and his gentleness, his pleasure in fishing and a
little rough shooting when the week's work was done, the sweet-
tempered and courteous manner in which he shouldered her affairs.
Mr Heelis would come over from Ambleside to see how the digging
and drainage were progressing, and if the weather were fine they would
take a walk together round the boundaries, or even up the hill and on

to the moor, from which they could look across the valley into West-morland. For Beatrix this new friendship was, among other things, an important link with Sawrey, for in the long winter months, when she could rarely get away from Bolton Gardens, his letters brought news of the progress of both farms. Hill Top was gradually expanding and doing well. As well as the Cannons, Miss Potter now employed a young dairy-maid and had even exhibited – whether cattle, pigs or sheep is not clear – at the Islington Agricultural Show. In Bolton Gardens, at Gwaynynog, on the weary round of seaside resorts, she thought longingly of Sawrey. 'I am very impatient to go up north,' she wrote from South Kensington early in the year, 'and plant a few more shrubs before things begin to bud.' A little later, having reached the Roscoes in Surrey on the trail of family visits, 'I . . . am going to Windermere with my parents next Wednesday. I have a doubt whether it is the best place for them so early in the year . . . Of course *I* shall like going because I can get over to Sawrey and see the new lambs.' And from lodgings in Sidmouth, where they spent a bitterly cold Easter, 'I wonder how my poor lambs are getting on, in the snow?'

The theme which now occupied her imagination was to do with the rocky crags and coppices around Sawrey, where foxes barked at night and the broad print of a badger could sometimes be seen on a muddy track through the bracken. It was to be her last-but-one Sawrey book, and a sinister masterpiece. Before beginning it, in the earlier months of 1911 she had dashed off, without a great deal of trouble, a book specially intended for her child-audience in America, from whom she now received so many letters that she sometimes had to dedicate a whole Sunday to answering them. *The Tale of Timmy Tiptoes* is an attractive story, and since the American grey squirrel has become the dominant species in our islands he has perhaps as much appeal for present-day children as Squirrel Nutkin. It may be prejudice that makes one think there is something lacking, and that studying grey squirrels and chipmunks at the Zoo is not the same as watching the familiar nut-gatherers around Esthwaite Water. I suspect that the squirrels and chipmunks in the book lived in the Small Mammals House, and that the bear who finally flushes Chippy Hackee out of his hollow tree inhabited the railed enclosure which preceded the Mappin Terraces.

What Beatrix Potter was really trying to do was to work out a final rabbit-drama in the woods and rocks above Sawrey, where another of

Benjamin Bunny's litters would be kidnapped and a dog-fox and a badger would be the villains. This new book, Warnes decided, was to be in a somewhat different style from its predecessors – not in the large format of *Ginger and Pickles* but with a longer story, fewer colour plates and a preponderance of smaller pen-and-ink pictures. The volume would be fatter than the earlier ones, have a slightly different style of binding and would be issued as the first of a 'new series'. This change of style suited Beatrix Potter very well; she was no longer inclined to produce twenty-six or more coloured illustrations to each book, involving months of laborious work. Fifteen colour plates would do very nicely and she could be generous with the black-and-whites – one to almost every page of text, each framed in a line border and drawn with the strength and emphasis of a woodcut. She had roughly written out the story some time ago, and the book would be dedicated to her cousin Caroline's son, two-year-old William Francis Clark of Ulva.

The Tale of Mr Tod is very frightening, but this, as Beatrix Potter well knew, is by no means a disadvantage in a children's story. The victims are rabbits, not humans; no child is likely to be haunted with fear of either a badger or a fox. In the story they are each other's enemies, which is not always true in nature; but it is this twist which brings about the happy ending.

Beatrix Potter was certainly 'provoked' a good many years later by Graham Greene's teasing suggestion that 'At some time between 1907 and 1909 Miss Potter must have passed through an emotional ordeal which changed the character of her genius. It would be impertinent,' he suggested, 'to enquire into the nature of the ordeal. Her case is curiously similar to that of Henry James. Something happened which shook their faith in appearances.' This was the kind of intellectual joke that she did not appreciate. The simple fact was that for a change she had written a story about 'two disagreeable people', and if a tale is told from a rabbit's point of view it would be absurd to represent a fox or a badger as anything but menacing.

Many people identify Mr Tod – 'surely a very common name for fox? It is probably Saxon,' Miss Potter informed her publisher – with the sandy-whiskered gentleman who so narrowly missed making a meal of Jemima Puddle-duck. But at the end of *that* story, with Kep and his fox-hound colleagues in pursuit, there were 'most awful noises – barking, baying, growls and howls, squealing and groans. And nothing more was ever seen of that foxy-whiskered gentleman.' So it is reasonable to suppose that Mr Tod is a different fox, and a bad-tempered one at that, with none of the other's misleadingly smooth manners. 'Nobody could call Mr Tod "nice". The rabbits could not bear him; they could smell him half a mile off. He was of a wandering habit and . . . they never knew where he would be next.' He had half a dozen houses, all of them dark, secretive and unsavoury. The one with which the story is concerned was near the wood at the top of Bull Banks, on the hill behind Castle Farm. 'This house was something between a cave, a prison and a tumble-down pig-stye. There was a strong door, which was shut and locked.'

The frontispiece to The Tale of Mr Tod. *'Nobody could call Mr Tod "nice" '.*

While Mr Tod is making his furtive rounds another, and deceptively amiable, character appears. 'Tommy Brock was a short bristly fat waddling person with a grin; he grinned all over his face. He was not nice in his habits. He ate wasps' nests and frogs and worms; and he waddled about by moonlight, digging things up.' He drops in on old

A study of Tommy Brock which, though in the
style of the small black-and-white drawings in the text,
did not actually appear in The Tale of Mr Tod.

Mr Benjamin Bouncer, who has been left in charge of a new litter of rabbit babies, while his son and daughter-in-law, Benjamin and Flopsy, are out. They smoke and drink together, coughing and laughing, until Mr Bouncer dozes off and Tommy Brock discreetly leaves the pre-mises. 'When Flopsy and Benjamin came back – old Mr Bouncer woke up. Tommy Brock and all the young rabbit babies had disappeared!'

Now follows a near-tragedy even more distressing than Tom Kit-ten's narrow escape from murder in the chimney. Tommy Brock, his sack full of baby rabbits, has forced his way into Mr Tod's rock-bound hide-out, shut up the little creatures in the brick oven and climbed into Mr Tod's bed to sleep off the effect of Flopsy's cowslip wine. Here he is eventually tracked by Benjamin Bunny and his cousin Peter, who fol-low his scent to the den at sunset. 'The setting sun made the window panes glow like red flame; but the kitchen fire was not alight. It was neatly laid with dry sticks, as the rabbits could see . . . Benjamin sighed with relief. But there were preparations upon the kitchen table which made him shudder. There was an immense empty pie-dish of blue willow pattern, and a large carving-knife and fork, and a chopper. At the other end of the table was a partly unfolded tablecloth, a plate, a tumbler, a knife and fork, salt-cellar, mustard and a chair – in short, preparations for one person's supper. No person was to be seen, and no young rabbits. The kitchen was empty and silent; the clock had run down. Peter and Benjamin flattened their noses against the window, and stared into the dusk . . .' At this ominous point in the story, with the baby rabbits imprisoned in the oven and the fox's earth apparently impregnable, the adult reader may notice a curious discrepancy. 'The sun had set; an owl began to hoot in the wood. There were many unpleasant things lying about, that had much better have been buried; rabbit bones and skulls, and chickens' legs and other horrors. It was a shocking place, and very dark.' But if we peer in at the murky window, as Peter and Benjamin are doing, we see a tidy farmhouse kitchen that would have done credit to Mrs Tittlemouse. There is a fresh-looking tablecloth, an eighteenth-century dining-room chair and a grandfather clock straight out of Hill Top. Something in Beatrix Potter's tidy nature had made it too difficult for her to depict squalor.

It is possible, too, from the naturalist's point of view, to question her characterisation of Tommy Brock. Badgers will certainly eat baby rabbits if they come across them, being more or less omnivorous, but they are clean animals, regularly turning out and airing the bedding from their own setts. I have never heard of a badger moving into a fox's earth, where the scent is always overpowering, although foxes are known to make casual use of other people's burrows. But badger-watching is an uncomfortable nocturnal pastime and was probably never thought of in Beatrix Potter's day, before the era of serious badger-research by naturalists and professional zoologists, so her portrayal of the brock's habits is to some extent less exact than her other delineations.

All this, of course, makes no difference to the power of the story, which reaches a climax of suspense when Mr Tod arrives in a very bad temper at his own dwelling and Peter and Benjamin are cowering in the burrow they have dug in desperation under the kitchen. Mr Tod's

impracticable plan for murdering Tommy Brock is a humiliating
failure, and their final confrontation ends in a battle so violent that
Beatrix Potter found difficulty in drawing it and finally solved the problem by making the kitchen dark. When the two enemies, biting and
snarling, roll out through the door and bump downhill over the rocks,
the rabbits make a lightning dash to the oven and rescue the prisoners –
'scuttering away down Bull Banks, half carrying, half dragging a sack
between them, bumpetty bump over the grass.' The horror is over;
we can return with relief to the rabbit-hole, where old Mr Bouncer is
in disgrace and Flopsy 'had been having a complete turn out and spring-
cleaning, to relieve her feelings.' Harmony is restored. The rabbit
babies, 'rather tumbled and very hungry', are fed and put to bed. Mr
Bouncer, somewhat upon his dignity after his recent disgrace, is presented with a new pipe and some fresh rabbit-tobacco, and they all have

Peter and Benjamin on their way through the wood,
tracking Mr Tod to his lair. One of Beatrix Potter's most
accomplished and beautifully composed pictures

dinner while Peter and Benjamin tell their story – 'but they had not waited long enough to be able to tell the end of the battle between Tommy Brock and Mr Tod.'

Does the final sentence suggest that Miss Potter was considering a sequel? If so, it was never written. She was almost at the end of the magically fertile period that had produced her best work and already her interest was turning in other directions. But she had no misgivings about the success of *Mr Tod*, which both in text and illustration exhibits her at her powerful best. Her only regret was over the endpapers, which she had been persuaded to do for the so-called 'new series of the *Peter Rabbit* books.' Now that they were printed in colour they looked like an advertisement, the very idea of which she abhorred. ('I have a most intense dislike to advertisement, and I have got on quite well enough without it.') 'I think the endpapers spoil the book,' she wrote rather crossly to Harold Warne. 'To my candid thinking, they are perfectly horrid – too big, and rather commonplace . . . They are just like the field advertisements along the railway lines. It never struck me when I was doing them. I am ashamed of them.'

The autumn of 1912, when *Mr Tod* was published, had been an anxious one for a very different reason. The friendship with William Heelis had become something more important, and he had brought the matter to a climax by proposing marriage. The few years' difference in their ages was of no consequence; at forty-six Beatrix Potter still had much of the freshness that had made her attractive as a girl; plump, blue-eyed, rosy-cheeked, with crisp wavy hair and a wholly unaffected manner, she was clearly intended by nature for a happy and unpretentious married life, which was what Willie Heelis was now modestly offering her. There was on her part no doubt at all about the suitability of the match; they were already 'very much attached' and the life he was offering was a continuation of all that she loved best. But what about her parents?

Her father was in wretched health – slowly dying of cancer, though this was not yet known – and her mother was having servant troubles and not in the best of tempers. Still, they had to be told, and Beatrix nerved herself for the confession. The result was as she had expected. She was to give Mr Heelis a firm refusal. A country solicitor, indeed!

The argument was painful and prolonged, dying down at last into mutterings and silence when Beatrix fell ill with influenza which turned into pneumonia, and her heart gave warning signals. Bertram had appeared suddenly from Scotland on a brief visit, and being taken into her confidence had astounded his parents with the revelation that he himself had been happily married for the past eleven years. Caroline Clark, too, receiving a despairing letter, had sent a characteristically bracing reply. 'I advised her to marry him quietly, in spite of them,' she told me many years later; 'they thought a country solicitor much beneath them . . . and she had the (now) old-fashioned ideas of duty from children to parents, and to excuse them wrote, "I see their objections, as we belong to the Bar and the Bench." '

At last, grudgingly, the objections were withdrawn, and by the spring of 1913 Beatrix was (more or less) allowed to consider herself engaged. Her health began slowly to mend. 'I cannot give you any idea at present when I shall be about again,' she wrote to Harold Warne in February. 'My temperature is about normal now, but the bronchitis is slow to move and the weather is not helpful.' By April she was well enough to accompany her parents to the Lakes, and immediately took refuge at Hill Top, from which, with Mr Heelis's help, she was able to supervise the conversion of Castle Cottage. This whitewashed farm-house dwelling, larger and less primitive than Hill Top, was to be their home when they were married. 'The weather is still very bad,' she wrote to Harold Warne. 'I seem to get on very slowly, I am decidedly stronger and look perfectly well, but I was completely stopped by a short hill on trying to walk to the next village this afternoon. I believe persevering slow exercise is the best cure; I do not think there is anything wrong with my heart now. I am always better on fine days when I can work in the garden.' To Millie Warne she wrote more frankly, for in these difficult days her old love for Norman was not forgotten. 'Norman was a saint,' she wrote, 'if ever man was good. I do not believe he would object . . . I am certainly not doing it from thoughtless light-heartedness as I am in very poor spirits about the future. We are very much attached and I have every confidence in w.h., but I think it can only mean waiting and I shall never be surprised if it was for the time broken off.'

The best possible therapy during these months of indecision and anxiety was that she was working on a new book, the last she would ever write about the village she loved. Her marriage and the independence it brought her were soon to complete her transformation into a new person, Mrs Heelis of Sawrey, farmer and landowner, whose deteriorating sight and involvement in country matters would bring the brief flowering of her small but authentic genius to an end.

The scene of the new story was her own farmyard; the characters her own pigs, for which she fully shared John Cannon's proud enthusiasm; the plot, despite its sinister overtones, 'the nearest' – once more I quote Graham Greene – 'the nearest Miss Potter had approached to a conventional love story.' This last was no doubt more accident than design, for, as usual, the theme had been in her mind for some time and she longed to invent something about her prize-winning pigs, particularly the 'six pink cherubs' with which her favourite sow regularly presented her. There was also a small black one, a 'little girl-pig' which she had bought from a neighbouring farmer against Cannon's wishes because she had been unable to resist her. So the characters she needed were all to hand – Aunt Pettitoes the sow, Alexander and Pigling Bland of the latest litter, and the little black stranger from another farm who fell in with their adventures.

Beatrix Potter's attitude towards the fate of her farm animals was a curiously mixed one. She could be immensely fond of them as individuals, yet switch at once to the practical view when the time came for sending them to market. This was sensible, of course; anyone who is squeamish about the slaughter of animals had better not be a farmer. But at least in the story she liked to think that Pigling Bland and Pigwig would escape (even though she was sending baby pork to her publishers for Christmas), so the two boy pigs are sent off to the local market and Beatrix Potter for once introduces herself into the pictures, giving Pigling Bland his market licence and seeing off the pair from the front porch of Hill Top. 'I pinned the papers, for safety, inside their waistcoat pockets; Aunt Pettitoes gave to each a little bundle, and eight conversation peppermints' – are these still available, I wonder? – 'with appropriate moral sentiments in screws of paper. Then they started.'

The watercolour drawing on the
opposite page, inscribed 'Nov. 19, 1909',
provided the background for
the frontispiece to The Tale of
Pigling Bland, published in 1913.
The watercolour on the right
is a variant of the frontispiece used
in the book.

' "Aunt Pettitoes, Aunt Pettitoes!
you are a worthy person, but your
family is not well brought up" . . .
"Yus, Yus!" sighed Aunt Pettitoes.
"And they drink bucketfuls of milk".'
This is a duplicate of the
illustration in Pigling Bland.
Hill Top is in the background.

Alexander, the silly one, soon loses his licence, is intercepted by the village policeman and led back to the farm. Pigling Bland goes mournfully on his way, loses himself in a wood and eventually creeps for shelter into a derelict shed which turns out to be a henhouse, so falling into the hands of Mr Piperson, a dishonest and disagreeable small farmer. (His kitchen, however, when Pigling Bland finds himself left alone there, turns out to be remarkably neat and tidy, with good furniture – another example of the Mrs Tittlemouse syndrome.) The heroine, Pig-wig, 'a perfectly lovely little black Berkshire pig' whom Piperson has stolen, is released by Pigling Bland from the kitchen cupboard, and the two plan their escape, stealing out from the house before daylight, and after some more nerve-racking adventures scampering over the county border to freedom. 'The sun rose while they were crossing the moor, a dazzle of light over the tops of the hills. The sunshine crept down the slopes into the peaceful green valleys, where little white cottages nestled in gardens and orchards. "That's Westmorland," said Pig-wig.'

The view in the little pen–and–ink sketch, like everything else in the book, belongs to Sawrey. 'The portrait of two pigs arm-in-arm – looking at the sunrise –' she wrote to a friend when the book was finished, 'is not a portrait of me and Mr Heelis, though it is a view of where we used to walk on Sunday afternoons. When I want to put William into a book, it will have to be some very tall thin animal.'

In spite of her demurely humorous denial, one is tempted to see a link between the happy escape of Pigling Bland and the approaching change in her own life. It is a nice coincidence that the book was published, and Beatrix Potter married, in the same month – October 1913.

(opposite) Beatrix and Mr Heelis at Bolton Gardens on their wedding-day

From then on, after a honeymoon spent in – well, of course! – Sawrey, her life changes as suddenly as a transformation scene. Hill Top is kept as it was, too small and primitive for their shared life; she was, besides, unwilling to have it changed. It remained her private retreat where she could keep books and papers, accumulate furniture and small treasures bought in country sales, and spend quiet hours alone when she had the leisure. The magic years of creating her own inimitable fantasies were at an end, and she embraced a new practical down-to-earth existence with all her accustomed energy and intelligence. True, a number of little books continued to appear over the years, but, with the exception of *Johnny Town-Mouse*, these were all pieced together from drawings and stories done many years before and now concocted into productions of dwindling merit, largely to satisfy her publishers. 'You will have to get used to the idea that my eyes are giving way,' she wrote sharply to Fruing Warne, 'whether you like it or not.'

The imaginative urge, too, had suddenly faded. Now that she was no longer alone, dependent on her own fantasies for amusement, the work that had meant so much to her lost its appeal. *Pigling Bland*, twenty years after she had written it, she dismissed as 'morbid . . . a pot-boiler made up when I was in bed with pneumonia.'

'The earlier books,' she wrote to a friend in her old age, '. . . were written in picture-letters of scribbled pen-and-ink for real children; but I confess that afterwards I painted most of the little pictures mainly to please myself. The more spontaneous the pleasure, the more happy the result. I cannot work to order; and when I had nothing more to say I had the sense to stop.'

Mrs Heelis of Sawrey was no longer the Beatrix Potter of the old days: she had become a different person, and the story of what she achieved in her new character I have related in another place.

THE GHOST OF
BEATRIX POTTER

Most of the hallowed books of childhood lose something of their magic as we grow older. Beatrix Potter's never. She even, to the mature eye, reveals felicities and depths of irony which pass the childish reader by; the dewy freshness of her landscape recalls Constable; her animals, for all the anthropomorphism of their dress and behaviour, show an imaginative fidelity to nature, a microscopic truth that one finds in the hedgerow woodcuts of Thomas Bewick.

It would be unwise to say any of this if she were still alive. She died in 1943, her brief creative period (thirteen years in all) having come to a close some thirty years before, since when she had evolved into a rather crusty and intimidating person, interested mainly in acquiring land and breeding Herdwick sheep, and whom nothing annoyed more than to have her books appraised on a critical level.

Graham Greene, as we have seen, was sharply rebuked when he wrote an essay in which he discussed the period of the 'great comedies' – *Tom Kitten*, *The Pie and the Patty-pan*, *Tiggy-Winkle* – and the subsequent 'dark period' of *The Roly-Poly Pudding* and *Mr Tod*, the 'near-tragedies,' using the tone of a sober scholar discussing Shakespeare.

Miss Potter was affronted. Nothing, she told him in a 'somewhat acid letter,' had disturbed her at the time of writing *Mr Tod* save the after-effects of 'flu, which had not altered her so-called genius in any way. She sharply deprecated any examination of her work by the 'Freudian school' of criticism. Yet the essay, despite its Gioconda smile, was a flattering one, and anybody but the author of *Peter Rabbit* would have been pleased. She had become, indeed, curiously ambivalent about the whole of her *oeuvre*. On the one hand, though she enjoyed the matter-of-fact acceptance of children, she was irritated to fury by any considered appraisal of her work; yet at the same time she could not have enough of the adulation which came to her in her latter years from America. Though she would see no others she would welcome reverent strangers from America, and the two or three poor-quality children's books of her late middle-age all went to American publishers and were not in her lifetime allowed to be printed in England. The reason for this, I believe, was that she was privately aware that they showed a sad falling-off, and while she was fairly confident of praise from the professional priestesses of 'kid lit.' in America she was unwilling to expose herself at home. Though she was impatient of serious attention from her compatriots, any hint of criticism exasperated her still more.

Miss Janet Adam Smith fell into this thorny trap in 1942 with an article in *The Listener*. 'Great rubbish, absolute bosh!' Beatrix Potter wrote to her publishers, who had thoughtfully sent her a copy, thinking she would be pleased to see herself placed, within her limits, in the 'same company as . . . Palmer, Calvert, Bewick and a host of earlier English artists.' To Miss Adam Smith she wrote that she had read the article with 'stupefaction'. Her wrath was increased by a humourless misconception, since she plainly thought she was being accused of copying these artists. Much taken aback, Miss Adam Smith hastened to reassure her, explaining that 'your illustrations often give the reader the same kind of pleasure as the pictures of these earlier artists,' and quoting a relevant passage from one of Constable's letters. Worse and worse. Miss Potter (or Mrs Heelis as she was then in private life) now thought she was accused of copying Constable, and replied with a long expostulatory letter, ending with the tart postscript, 'When a person has been nearly thirty years married it is not ingratiating to get an envelope addressed to "Miss." ' (An observation which would pass without comment in any of the several books about Tabitha Twitchit.)

I could, if asked, have warned anybody that it was unwise to meddle at all with Beatrix Potter, having nearly done so myself some time before, when I was very sharply sent about my business. Like most people who have been wholly entranced by her little books in infancy, I had long believed that Beatrix Potter was dead. The occasional new production that one came across in bookshops (*The Story of a Fierce Bad Rabbit*, for example) was so egregiously bad compared with the early masterpieces as to strengthen the suspicion that they were written by somebody else. The bookshops denied this, and were not believed. It was no good asking questions about Beatrix Potter, because at that time nobody knew anything about her.

It was about 1941 that I first discovered that she was still alive, and living in the Lake District. My stepdaughter was at school near Windermere, and brought home tempting scraps of some local legends that

Mrs William Heelis at Keswick Show

were current about her. She was very old. She was very rich. She was
a recluse. She was a little mad. She drove round the lake on Sundays in
an open carriage, wearing black lace and sitting very stiffly behind the
coachman. (This, it turned out, was a memory of her widowed mother
who had done exactly that.) Or, and this was the most popular legend
of all, she did labourer's work in the fields, wearing sacks and rags.

It was very puzzling, but at least it seemed undeniable that she was
still alive, and I fell, like Graham Greene and Miss Adam Smith soon

Sawrey under snow, seen from the Tower Bank Arms, 7 March 1909

after, into the innocent folly of wishing to write about her. Clearly, if she were as reclusive as people said, one must approach with care, and since it seemed desirable to go to the fountain-head as a precaution against inaccuracy or offence, I decided to write to her.

The sensible approach, indeed the only one, since I did not know where she lived, was through her publishers, and I wrote to Frederick Warne and Co. for her address. They replied with ill-concealed horror that on no account, in no circumstances, could her address be given. She lived in close retirement, she never saw anybody, they had her express instructions that nobody must ever be allowed to write her a letter.

This could have been final, but it was also rather a challenge to in-genuity, and since my intentions were of the most serious and respectful description I could not see why they should refuse to forward a letter. They did not refuse, though they clearly shrank from the impertinence, and in due course an extremely polite missive was forwarded to Sawrey. I told her of my lifelong pleasure in her books (addressing her, I am thankful to remember, as Mrs Heelis), expressed my admiration and my wish to write an essay on her work, and asked if I might call on her to check some facts and submit what I should write for her approval.

Back came, in a few days, the rudest letter I have ever received in my life. Certainly not, she said; nothing would induce her to see me. 'My books have always sold without advertisement, and I do not propose to go in for that sort of thing now.' Her reply could hardly have been more offensively worded if I had asked her to sponsor a deodorant advertisement.

Well, that was that, I thought. It would be impossible to write any-thing in the face of such hostility, a snub so out of proportion to the occasion. I tore up the letter in indignation, not knowing that I was only one of innumerable people who had had the breath knocked out of them by her acerbity.

And then, in 1943, she died; and Raymond Mortimer, at that time literary editor of the *New Statesman*, asked if I could write him an article on Beatrix Potter. I did my best, but it was a poor best, for no-body seemed to know anything about her and the crumbs of fact I could gather were contemptible. I knew only that she had lived and farmed for years in the Lake District and was the wife of a country solicitor. I had to confine myself to an appreciation of her work, and even this contained some sad inaccuracies.

It soon became apparent, from the meagre obituary notices which followed, that I was not the only one who had failed to find out anything. The tone, everywhere, was one of surprise that she had been so recently alive, and it was suddenly borne in on me that what I wanted to do was to write her biography. Alas for such optimism! Here was a life so innocent, so uneventful that one would have supposed the only difficulty would be in finding something to say. Yet, when I approached her widower, the gentlest of men, who received me with a trembling blend of terror and courtesy, it appeared that he considered himself under oath to conceal the very few facts that he had in his possession. He knew remarkably little about her life before their marriage, which had taken place when she was approaching fifty, and what he did know he was unwilling to divulge. He impressed me as a man who for thirty years had lived under the rule of a fairly dominant feminine authority, and whenever, reluctantly, he imparted a scrap of information or a date, he would glance apprehensively over his shoulder, as though every moment expecting the door to open. This impression of the balance in their relationship was later confirmed by – among other things – a letter she wrote to a friend a few years before her death, when she was in hospital for an operation. 'I am an old woman and tired. I am exceedingly sorry for my husband. You may have noticed I am the stronger half of the pair; moreover the money is mine, and death duties are so heavy that my death before his would be awkward.'

The house was indeed palpably haunted by her. She had not long been dead, and the imprint of her personality was on every chair and table. Her clothes still hung behind the door, her geraniums trailed and bloomed along the window-sill, her muddles lay unsorted at one end of the table while he took his meals at the other, even a half-eaten bar of chocolate with her teeth marks in it lay whitened and stale among the litter of letters on her writing table.

Yet he had expressed himself willing, after much patient argument, that a biography should be written, and as a man of honour truly believed that he was doing his best. He had been, it is true, quite implacable at first, and had been at pains to explain, with the most considerate politeness, why such a project was impossible. She would not have wished it, he said; what was more, she would never have

(opposite) Beatrix in the porch of Hill Top, 1943, a few months before her death

allowed it; and here he looked over his shoulder again and blew his nose in a large cotton handkerchief. The argument which finally convinced him, in spite of his obvious misgiving that agreement was treachery, was that sooner or later, either in England or America, a biography would be written, and it was perhaps better to have it written while he was still alive and could presumably exercise some control over the biographer. He seemed relieved to think that by this means he might escape the attentions of some frantic American, but I had to promise that every word of every line should be subject to his inspection, and left the cottage after that first interview with my point gained, in the deepest possible dejection.

I knew exactly what he had in mind; the sort of biography he had at last brought himself, after the most scrupulous searching of conscience, to consider. It would be about a quarter of an inch thick, bound in navy blue boards with gilt lettering, and would be called *A Memoir of the late Mrs William Heelis*. We did not discuss the point, but I am sure he took it for granted that it would be for private circulation.

Then began a series of evenings which we spent together and which I look back on with misery. Every question, however innocuous, was met with the frightened response, 'Oh, you can't mention *that*!' Any detail of her parents, the date of her birth, even the fact of her marriage to himself fell under this extraordinary prohibition. Night after night I stretched my tact and ingenuity to breaking-point, feverishly changing from subject to subject, retreating at once when I saw his poor eyes watering in alarm, creeping back each night to my cold bedroom at the Sawrey Inn to sleepless hours of knowing the whole thing to be impossible.

And then, after many evenings and by the merest accident, I changed my tune. Some tremulous negative, some futile protest over a harmless question, produced that sudden trembling which I have experienced only two or three times in my life and associate with the crisis known as losing one's temper. I found myself banging the table with clenched fist and crying 'Mr Heelis, you *must not obstruct me in this way*!' The moment it had happened, in the petrified silence, I was overcome with embarrassment. But the effect was magical. He jumped, looked over his shoulder again as towards a voice he knew, pulled himself together, blew his nose, apologized, and suddenly seemed to feel remarkably better. I had never meant to do it, but the inference was plain. Tact,

A view across Esthwaite Water, December 1913

compliance, the yielding deviousness that had cost me so much effort were things he was unaccustomed to and could not deal with. With decision, with firm opinion, he felt at home, and responded in the most eager and obliging manner. Pleased at last to be able to express his pride in his wife's fame he brought out his boxes of letters, rummaged in the bottoms of wardrobes and at the backs of drawers for photographs, produced such addresses and names as from time to time crossed his uncertain memory. The thing was started; I breathed a sigh of relief; though not without foreboding that my difficulties were only begun.

They were indeed, for over his eager compliance, which even extended to giving me two of her watercolours, hung the cloud of that final inspection of the manuscript which I knew would mar all. Left to himself, with typescript before him, I knew how his trembling hand would score it through, how little, how very little would come back to me actually unscathed, how in despair I would fling that 'little' into the wastepaper basket.

One of the last photographs ever taken of Beatrix Potter

Outside the precincts of Castle Cottage there was no such reticence; there were many people living who had known her well, Potter cousins, the niece of her governess, Miss Hammond, innumerable farm and cottage neighbours who thought of her only as the eccentric little figure that the Lake District remembers – the odd bundle of country clothing, clad in innumerable petticoats, full of good humour, of authority, of sudden acerbities which could flash out quite brutally and inflict hurts where she probably never intended them. 'I began to assert myself at seventy,' she wrote to one of her cousins a few months before she died, but this was an understatement. She had been asserting herself for thirty years, and the Lake District had come to respect her as a person it was dangerous to oppose, but very safe to love.

Those who spoke of her with the most feeling were the shepherds and farmers with whom she was most akin in temperament, and to the poetry of whose lives she had always responded, almost with the nostalgia of an exile. On her deathbed she had scribbled a note of indecipherable farewell to her old Scottish shepherd, the 'lambing-time man' who had come to her every spring for nearly twenty years, and with whom she had kept up a long and affectionate correspondence. He had preserved all her letters, dated and wrapped up in little parcels in the recesses of his cottage, and he sent them to me as an act of piety, for love of her memory.

I took innumerable journeys, sometimes with Mr Heelis, more often alone, over the fells and along the valleys, to cottages and farmhouses that she owned, talking to the people who had known her. She had been a workmanlike landlord, most practically interested in fences and gates, the felling and planting of timber, the repairing of walls. As a sheep-breeder she was knowledgeable and shrewd, and the farmers round about thought of her principally as a dangerous rival at sheep fairs and ram shows, an enigmatic and authoritative presence in the Keswick tavern where the Herdwick Sheep Breeders' Association held its meetings.

At the same time I embarked on a sea of correspondence, which ebbed and flowed for more than a year. Beatrix Potter, for all the crowded busyness of her later years, when she was managing a number of farms and doing important work for the National Trust in the Lake District, possessed that last-century sense of leisure which permitted her to write long and frequent letters to a great many people – sometimes even to people she had never met, but whose personalities, when they wrote to her, had taken her fancy. Now, these letters began to flow into my hands, not only from English senders, but from places as far afield as America and New Zealand; and the task of deciphering and sifting them for their shreds of biographical interest was for a time quite heavy.

To me, the series of letters which Warnes, her publishers for more than forty years, had kept without a gap since the day when they first accepted *Peter Rabbit*, was the most interesting of all, for they reflected her slow and painstaking development as an artist, her emotional growth from girl to woman, her emergence from unhappy and re-spectable nonentity into the kind of personality about whom biogra-phies are written. The Warne family had played an important, and more than professional part in her life, and without their help and confidence the book could never have been written.

But however much help I had from her publishers, relations, and other friends, there was still to be faced the final confrontation with Mr Heelis, when, as I privately guessed, he would bring up reinforcements of prohibition and his mandate would fall on everything I had written.

I remember that on my last evening in Sawrey, returning from a walk with which I had tried in vain to recruit my spirits, I found a penny lying at the foot of a stile and decided to toss for it; whether I should give it up there and then or write the book as I saw it and be prepared to forget it for years in a locked drawer. The penny said heads, and I put it in my pocket as a charm. The drawer was the thing. I did not know how old Mr Heelis was, nor how I should explain my curious delay; but I was resolved I would not expose myself, or him, to the long-drawn agony of his excisions.

As it turned out, the penny proved a true oracle, for the poor widower, left alone and at a loss without the mainstay on which his thoughts and decisions had so long depended, died a few months after, before the book was finished, and I never paid that final visit to Sawrey. I do not believe he turns in his grave, honest man, nor that the stout little ghost which haunts the place would still, after all this time, find it necessary to be angry.

THE BEATRIX POTTER BOOKS

(Published in English by F. Warne & Co. Ltd, unless otherwise stated)

1 The Tale of Peter Rabbit (privately printed, first edition, flat back),
    250 copies, Dec. 1901, followed by a second edition (round back,
    200 copies, Feb. 1902)
2 The Tale of Peter Rabbit 1902
3 The Tailor of Gloucester (privately printed, 500 copies) 1902
4 The Tale of Squirrel Nutkin 1903
5 The Tailor of Gloucester 1903
6 The Tale of Benjamin Bunny 1904
7 The Tale of Two Bad Mice 1904
8 The Tale of Mrs Tiggy-Winkle 1905
9 The Pie and the Patty-pan (first published in the larger format) 1905
10 The Tale of Mr Jeremy Fisher 1906
11 The Story of a Fierce Bad Rabbit (panoramic form) 1906
12 The Story of Miss Moppet (panoramic form) 1906
13 The Tale of Tom Kitten 1907
14 The Tale of Jemima Puddle-Duck 1908
15 The Roly-Poly Pudding (first published in the larger format). Later
    renamed The Tale of Samuel Whiskers 1908
16 The Tale of the Flopsy Bunnies 1909
17 Ginger and Pickles (first published in the larger format) 1909
18 The Tale of Mrs Tittlemouse 1910
19 Peter Rabbit's Painting Book 1911
20 The Tale of Timmy Tiptoes 1911
21 The Tale of Mr Tod 1912
22 The Tale of Pigling Bland 1913
23 Tom Kitten's Painting Book 1917
24 Appley Dapply's Nursery Rhymes (smaller format) 1917
25 The Tale of Johnny Town-Mouse 1918
26 Cecily Parsley's Nursery Rhymes (smaller format) 1922
27 Jemima Puddle-Duck's Painting Book 1925

28 Peter Rabbit's Almanac for 1929, 1928

29 The Fairy Caravan (privately printed, 100 copies) 1929

30 The Fairy Caravan (David McKay, Philadelphia) 1929. First English
edition, July 1952

31 The Tale of Little Pig Robinson (David McKay, Philadelphia) 1930

32 The Tale of Little Pig Robinson (larger format) 1930

33 Sister Anne (David McKay, Philadelphia) 1932

34 Wag-by-Wall (limited edition, 100 copies) 1944

35 Wag-by-Wall (The Horn Book, Boston) 1944

36 The Tale of the Faithful Dove (limited edition, 100 copies) 1955

37 The Art of Beatrix Potter 1955

38 The Tale of the Faithful Dove (F. Warne & Co. Inc., New York)
1956

39 The Journal of Beatrix Potter, 1881–1897 (transcribed from her
code-written manuscript) 1966

40 The Tailor of Gloucester – a facsimile of the original manuscript
and illustrations (limited edition, 1500 copies, F. Warne & Co.
Inc., New York) 1968

41 The Tailor of Gloucester – from the original manuscript (F. Warne
& Co. Inc., New York) 1968

42 The Tailor of Gloucester – from the original manuscript (the English
edition) 1969

43 The Tale of the Faithful Dove – with illustrations by Marie Angel
(F. Warne & Co. Inc., New York) 1970

44 The Tale of the Faithful Dove – with illustrations by Marie Angel
(English edition) 1971

45 The Writings of Beatrix Potter – a history of, including unpublished
work 1971

46 The Sly Old Cat 1971

47 The Tale of Tuppenny – with illustrations by Marie Angel (F. Warne
& Co. Inc., New York) 1973

48 The History of the Tale of Peter Rabbit 1976

Six of the *Tales* have been printed in braille by the Royal Institute for
the Blind. Fifteen of the *Tales* have been translated into French and
Japanese, thirteen into Dutch, twelve into Africaans, ten into Swedish,
nine into Norwegian, eight into Danish and German, five into Welsh,
two into Latin, and one into Italian and Spanish.

ILLUSTRATION ACKNOWLEDGMENTS

All the colour illustrations of watercolour drawings by Beatrix Potter have been reproduced from the originals. Grateful acknowledgment is made to the following libraries, museums and collections for giving facilities for photography or providing illustrations. The references given are to the pages of the book.

The British Museum 108 right, 174

Mrs Winifred Boultbee 121

Crown Copyright, reproduced with the permission of the Controller of Her Majesty's Stationery Office, and the Director, Royal Botanic Gardens, Kew 45

Kensington and Chelsea Public Libraries 13, 16

Mrs S. M. Manson 112

Miss Marjorie Moore 64, 68

The National Book League (Leslie Linder Collection) 38, 41 below, 52, 76, 87, 90, 95, 98, 154, 162, 194, 195 above

The National Trust (Beatrix Potter Museum at Hill Top, Sawrey) 3, 8, 10, 11, 17, 19, 20, 24, 28, 31, 32, 33, 43, 44, 51, 56, 57, 60, 62 below right, 73 right, 73 below, 75, 78, 96, 97, 102, 106, 110, 119, 122 below, 125, 126, 130, 131, 135 above, 143, 146, 151 below, 159, 163 below, 167, 169, 171 above, 187, 190, 201, 208

A. & F. Pears Limited 59

Rare Book Department, Free Library of Philadelphia 107

The Rainbird Publishing Group (illustration by Colin Twinn) 120

The Tate Gallery, London 58, 82, 83, 101, 107

Victoria and Albert Museum, London 1, 2, 5, 7, 14, 15, 21, 22, 23, 25, 26, 27, 34, 35, 36, 37, 41 above, 42, 46, 47, 48, 54, 55, 62 above and below left, 63, 66 above and below, 73 left, 74, 80, 99, 100, 114, 118, 122 above, 124, 129, 134, 135 below, 137, 139, 144, 145, 149, 150-1, 151 above right, 154, 156, 158 above and below, 160, 161, 163 above, 164, 165, 166 above and below, 168, 171 below, 178, 179, 182, 188, 195 below, 197, 202, 205, 207

Index